ANX & US

Thirteen approaches to
a universal issue

Compiled by Carolyn Street

2020 Youier Media

Copyright © 2020 by Carolyn Street

All rights reserved. This book or any portion thereof may not be reproduced or used in any manner whatsoever without the express written permission of the publisher except for the use of brief quotations in a book review or scholarly journal.

First Printing: 2020

ISBN 9781999710699

Youier Media
80 Queen Victoria Road
Llanelli, SA15 2TH
YouierMedia.com

Contents

Introduction … 5
Healing Anxiety With Intuitive Painting … 7
Helping Myself Through Anxiety … 21
The Irrationality Of Batman … 35
Dealing With Anxiety To ToastMasters … 49
The Anxiety Mindset … 57
The Gift Of Anxiety … 81
Thanxiety … 103
Treating Anxiety In Others … 117
A Hero's Journey … 139
The Medicine Of The Future Is Sound … 163
Be Your Own "Emotional Electrician" … 187
Youier, The Ultimate Happiness Hack! … 207
Using Ayurveda To Heal Anxiety … 231
Now What? … 259
Sadness And Us … 261
Acknowledgments … 262
Youier Media … 264

Introduction

How do you ask for help when it feels impossible to articulate what's going on inside your own head? When one day can feel easy and the exact same circumstances on a different day send you into a downward spiral? Add isolation, guilt and self-condemnation into the mix and is it any surprise that anxiety has become this thing that no-one really wants to talk about?

We think it's just us, that no-one can really understand how we feel or why we feel what we feel. We don't even understand it ourselves so how can we possibly expect anyone else to get it?

The truth is anxiety is never just you. You are not alone.

We are 12 artists, working professionals, coaches and therapists, all experienced experts with anxiety, be it our own or loved ones' friends' and clients'. *Anxiety And Us* comprises our personal stories and the learnings we discovered in our individual quests to turn anxiety around from an adversary to an ally.

We are diverse in culture, background and life experiences and our hope is that this book will help bring relief from anxiety so people can attain self-love from a fresh and refreshing set of perspectives.

It's time to shine a light into the dark places of anxiety and come together to heal and grow.

Photographs and illustrations to support the book can be found in the accompanying Facebook group, Anxiety And Us, where you'll also find audio versions of each chapter read by the author.

Fun fact: The cover is yellow because yellow corresponds to worry and anxiety in the Japanese Jin Shin Jyutsu (R) modality that incorporates numerous ancient and scientific traditions.

Each volume in the *And Us* series is organised according to the attitudes (states) classified by JSJ. Anxiety encompasses shame, guilt, embarrassment, overthinking, appetite, boundaries, preferences and the associated flavour is sweet. Diabetes is the associated critical label.

- Carolyn Street, August 2020

Healing Anxiety With Intuitive Painting
by Kellie Ahl

Part 1: Identify what's running the show

As I begin to write this Chapter, I am riddled with anxiety. To be specific, I am riddled with shame.

Who am I to write a chapter for an actual book? I am not a writer. My grammar is appalling. My English homework had big red lines through it with "waffle" written on it and "grammar!!!" in the margins. I have no idea how to write so many words anymore…..

Throughout my life I have I have experienced anxiety in its various forms. My triggers ranged from panic attacks over school exams to the fear of public speaking to PTSD-related anxiety after the horrific death of my father.

Until recently I would have argued that I didn't have any notable shame within me that I had been unconscious of, and, it wasn't until I finally acknowledged and accepted the toxic shame within me that I realised I had only ever been learning to deal with the symptoms of anxiety.

Whilst the numerous tools I have learnt over the years have been invaluable at helping me manage my anxiety they did not, as I desired, serve to heal the root cause so I'd like to steer this conversation about alleviating anxiety holistically to healing toxic shame holistically.

Toxic shame is the deep-rooted, dark, murky, most suppressed emotion of the very lowest vibration. It is at the root of most fear, anxiety, frustration, anger, grief and sadness we harbour. It is not to be confused with guilt or embarrassment.

Many of us are carrying it around unconsciously. It drags us down and pulls us back like invisible ankle chains. It is insidious. It hides in every area of our life; in our thoughts, our emotions, our body, our behaviours and beliefs.

It will show up in disguise in our relationships, in our work, in our health, in our inability to move forward to achieve our goals and follow our dreams. It can be hard to find and even more difficult to process.

Its narrative runs on repeat; "You're not good enough.", "Who do you think you are?", "You are bad". But we're often not even conscious of it.

This deep rooted shame story will trigger our anxiety and leave us in fight, flight or freeze mode preventing any attempts we make outwardly to move forward.

When we unconsciously live from this place time and time again we will get to the brink of what will move us forward in one or more areas of our life and either ourselves, or something outside of us, will sabotage our ability to take the next step.

This of course will lead to more anxiety and more judgements of our character and self-worth further validating, whilst disguising, our shame.

We may conclude that the very real and crippling effects of anxiety along with other reasons within ourselves are the primary cause of our inability to move forward. But once we begin the journey to face our toxic shame, with love and compassion, we come to realise that it is the driving force of our unconscious sabotaging beliefs and behaviours.

In the light of this awareness we can begin to understand our anxiety as our body's way of letting us know that something deeper is needing healing and it becomes not the beast to be feared that it once was. So how do we heal shame?

According to Law of Attraction teachers Abraham-Hicks in their book "Ask and It Is Given", our emotions are precise indicators of the vibration we are projecting to the world and everything we attract in our life is a result of our vibration (our frequency or energy). They outlined an Emotional Guidance Scale which sequences our feelings and emotions from those with the highest vibration to the lowest.

Shame lies at the bottom of this scale with grief, anxiety, unworthiness, powerlessness, depression, despair and insecurity. Therefore to move up the emotional scale we must focus our healing here by bringing the light of awareness on our feelings of shame. We need to get curious about what, when and where are the triggers and how it feels in our body, and watch how life can open up before our very eyes.

In her TED Talk "Listening to Shame", Brené Brown speaks of empathy as the antidote to healing shame and indeed "me too" is how we can powerfully support each other. Being honest with ourselves and others about our feelings will help us to heal ourselves and societal shame that is epidemic in our culture.

Learning to honour oneself; to see ourselves as sovereign - meaning to have integrity and be in control of one's own body and life - allows us to know that it's OK to feel shame (or any low vibration emotion) so we may express it and thereby transmute its energy.

But how do we begin the journey into shame when we are unsure how to even feel it? How can we identify shame within ourself when it's so damn sneaky?

It is true that some people do not feel a deep sense of shame and who have not taken on such negative fundamental beliefs about themselves but I would invite anyone who struggles with anxiety to explore this emotion and how it might be running a narrative within themselves and playing out in their life.

As an artist I use paint to get curious and down and dirty with all my emotions especially with those I'd rather not face such as shame. Painting is a safe way to enable us to feel and move emotions through our body; to honour and accept them so that they will reveal the wisdom they want us to know.

Let me be clear that I am not an art therapist nor have I had any personal experience of formal art therapy. Using paint to transmute energy within me has evolved through my embracing an intuitive painting process; allowing my intuition and my body's feelings and emotions to be the source of my inspiration.

Paint allows us to boldly go where few dare and to express ourself physically and emotionally in healthy ways. No one will get hurt in the name of our expedition into shame or what Carl Jung termed the "swampland of the soul". Through the process of painting in this way we can receive answers from deep within our inner being that our minds' cannot begin to fathom.

We do not have to identify as a creative to work with paint and I urge you to try it and see. Below is my simple painting process to express and transmute shame. It is a quest worth undertaking because once uncovered and honoured shame can be transmuted in the greatest gift for transformation: Your power.

You will come to know and own your Sovereignty.

Love will flow through and to you.

Freedom will be yours.

Part 2: Healing shame (all emotions) with intuitive painting

Stage 1 - Painting shame

Feel into your toxic shame. Listen to your ego's negative voice, when and where in your life do you tell yourself you are fundamentally bad/wrong/not good enough etc. How do these words make you feel? Where do you feel the response in your body? There's no need to go deep into past experiences.

Note: If you struggle to locate shame just use your imagination: Ask yourself if you had deep toxic shame how would you feel? Where would you feel it? What might it look like? E.g. heavy, dark, cold, sad or does it conjure feelings of anxiety - increased heart and breath rate, raise in temperature, butterflies in stomach etc.

You may wish to play some music to help reflect the feelings. Get a large sheet of paper or ideally a canvas and some black paint.

Using your finger or a brush write "SHAME" in big letters on your canvas then continue to write words or phrases or paint symbols and marks that describe/represent the feeling of shame or the thoughts or images that underlie it. It doesn't matter if you can't read your writing or see the images and it all becomes a mess. Allow the energy to flow, be spontaneous, keep moving, work quickly and feel the energy of shame behind it.

Choose a few more colours that represent the different aspects of shame you have felt into and begin to blend and spread the paint in any way that feels good to your body using your hands (on any part of your body!), brushes, sponges, rollers, rags or stamps.

Allow your attention to focus into your body. Where do you feel shame? How does it want to move through you?

Allow your whole body to move as you work the paint if it feels right.

Close your eyes, and locate the body sensations. Paint with your eyes closed if it feels good to you. You may feel inspired to scribble and scratch into the paint, to wipe or wash large areas of paint away.

I thoroughly recommend the cathartic practice of spraying the paint with water and watch it run down the canvas. (Note: this can get very messy!).

If you get 'stuck', turn your canvas 90 degrees or upside down allow the paint to run in different directions or paint with your eyes closed.

The only rule is DO NOT QUESTION YOUR INTUITIVE GUIDANCE on how or what to paint! Just paint! Your mind is of no value here. This is all about feelings and body sensations. The result is equally irrelevant even if you have a big murky mess!

There are no mistakes. You cannot do this wrong.

This is a freeing and liberating exercise. Tears may flow, anger may surface or you may simply enjoy the process. All emotions are welcome. Again do not question your emotions or your ability. Keep focusing on the paint and let everything move as you feel guided to by your own body's wisdom.

When you feel you finished this part of the process, stop and allow your painting to dry. Well done! Your first step to transmuting shame is complete.

Stage 2 - Mediate/Commune with your painting

Daily if possible, write in a journal.

How did the process of painting shame feel? Where did you feel it? Did it bring up old memories or an awareness of how it shows up in your life? What is its narrative?

With this awareness of shame, what would feel like the opposite of shame for you? Is it unconditional love? Acceptance? Empathy? Honouring your Sovereignty and your Power? When you think of this empowered feeling where do you feel it? What is the sensation?

Continue to commune with your painting daily in whatever way feels good for you as you. Live with it in your space. Allow it to breathe; to take up space; to speak to you. This will enhance the effects of the experience and allow it to reveal it's wisdom to you. You may wish to make notes in your journal or speak out loud to your painting whatever feels right to you, trust that, it is key to the process.

I usually allow a period of days before I move onto the next stage but sometimes it's as soon as the canvas is dry and others its weeks. Again allow your body to tell you when it's ready to move on to the next stage. You'll get the urge. You'll know.

Stage 3 - Transmuting shame

Consider the empowered feeling that you identify as the opposite of shame for you. You are now going to offer this energy to your canvas.

Allow this feeling to guide you in choosing your next colour choices. Don't question yourself, pick two or three colours. TIP: I recommend selecting colours in either the warm (reds, oranges and yellows) or cool range (blues, greens, purples) so that you don't muddy your colours unintentionally.

Again you may wish to choose some music that reflects the feelings you wish to invoke but silence may be equally compelling.

Begin to work the colours onto your shame layer. You do not have to cover the entire canvas or first layer completely. You may wish to allow some to be seen through to add contrast and depth to this next layer and as a way of honouring the healthy expression of your dark side. Again, do what feels right to you.

Move your body. Close your eyes if you wish. Allow the paint to flow through you. Use any of the tips in Stage 1 to keep the paint moving.

DO NOT QUESTION YOUR IMPULSES.
DO NOT JUDGE WHAT'S HAPPENING.

BE INTENTIONAL about channeling these higher vibration emotions through the paint onto your canvas.

ALLOW your painting to be your medicine and it will be.

Stop when you feel you are finished.

As you contemplate the finished work, write down any emotions and insights that have to come you through this painting process.

Stage 4 - Honour your painting

Your painting is MAGIC! It will reveal its deeper wisdom to you over time and remind you to shift both your perception and experience of anxiety.

Live with your Transmuted Shame painting and commune with it daily in meditation or via your journal to glean its wisdom. Ask it questions. It is your tool, your guide.

Healing anxiety through healing shame

It is my highest intention that in sharing my painting process, it will serve as an empowering process for you to honour all parts of yourself; to express and transform shame by bringing it into the light in a safe, healthy and fun way.

This will help you to step into your personal power to become the creator of your life and healing therefore reducing the triggers and symptoms of anxiety.

About Kellie Ahl

Kellie is an intuitive expressionist artist based in Hertfordshire who specialises in teaching her painting process to anyone who is curious by facilitating workshops & retreats, 121 sessions and leading her transformational Creative Women's Circles. In addition to her personal work, she also paints live at private events and creates powerful personal pieces of commissioned art to put the stamp of your soul in your home.

She passionately believes we were all born to paint because it is the language of our body and soul and a powerful way to access, express and transmute our emotions, subconscious thoughts and behaviour patterns and bring about change we desire. More about Kellie and her work can be found at www.kellieahl.com or follow her on instagram @kellieahl1.

Helping Myself Through Anxiety
by Maybelline Tan

Anxiety is like having a list of todos, worrying and wondering when they will ever end and how to resolve them. The thoughts in my head go around in loops and at times I feel that I have no control over them.

The voices appear not to be mine, I don't know where these voices in my head come from. One thing is for sure, they are harsh, critical, demanding and relentless. When Anxiety becomes a part of me, it feels like I am Anxiety and that this is normal. I no longer differentiate between the voices within me or to see another way to treat myself more kindly. But anxiety happens in stages and it doesn't get better and the more I allow it, the more it festers.

One day when I was on a train, I thought of my bills, sales target, duty as a filial daughter to bring enough bread home for my ageing parents, the client who was demanding a proposal from me and another one whom I needed to create a proposal for. I had to find out how to convince him why my product is better. Oh yes and the angry one who rants whenever he answers his phone..the list of worries and todos went on. Suddenly, I felt like I was almost going to have a heart attack. My heart was palpitating, it was painful and I was sweating. I clutched my chest and I noticed myself gasping for air, almost as though I was choking. That was the first time I experienced a panic attack. The attacks became more and more frequent and they were hard to predict. I could be walking on the street while ruminating over my usual list and an attack would happen.

Some mornings, I did not want to wake up. I dreaded the day ahead and life felt purposeless. Mornings were a dread. I would be crying to my then-boyfriend, begging him to hold my hand to take me to the toilet because I was scared. I wasn't sure what was I afraid of. I had to mentally convince myself to place a foot on the ground daily when I get out of my bed. That was the one conversation in my head that helped me. "Just put one foot down, one at a time, you can do it Maybelline." I had to cheer myself on because my ex-boyfriend couldn't comprehend what was going on within me. I had no clue myself. Then nights came and I would dread going to bed because I knew that once I fell sleep, I would wake up the next day with the same thing happening. I wished to drag my nights, as though not sleeping could prevent another day from happening. The morning self-motivation was somewhat useful but this cycle continued, and the panic attacks rose to 5-6 times a day. Naive me thought that I might have a heart disease! I booked an appointment with a cardiologist and had a detailed round of checks. He asked me some questions, listened to my heartbeat and took my blood pressure. He said my heart seemed fine and he let me off. He didn't suggest that it was a panic attack either but he said I was probably just too stressed out.

Some days I felt really sad for no apparent reason and I'd find myself crying non-stop. I would feel like crying from nowhere. In the middle of a train ride, while walking to work, while waiting for the bus or scrolling through my social media feed. It got to a point I felt that no one in this world understood me and I questioned my existence. I kept looking at the stars above in the skies. Every night when walking home, I would stare into the skies high above me and wish that I was somewhere but here on this Earth. "Take me," I thought. "I'm too sensitive and vulnerable to this world. Why am I made this way? Why do I cry these endless tears? Why am I feeling so much? What's wrong with me?" I broke down many times in a state of overwhelmed emotions and the more I cried, the more anxious and out of breath I became. My chest hurt and I hyperventilated. One of those nights, I decided that I was going to die but something inside me was afraid to go. I needed help. I knew then I really needed help for someone to save me. I was afraid of what I might do to myself. So I called my only confidant, my ex-boyfriend. "Please help me, I think I'm going to die and I don't know how to stop these thoughts. Please," I said.

He told me coldly that he didn't know what he could do. His tone was a mixture of helplessness and frustration. Even he couldn't help me, I thought. In that split second, something just clicked within me. It was the voice that said, "Looks like only I can help myself now."

Truth is, I didn't want to die back then, I had no courage to. I could hear my father's voice in the bedroom next door and I knew it would break his heart if I was gone. I had two clear realisations that saved me that night. 1, I don't want to hurt my dad and 2, cowardice to face death. It wasn't in my awareness at that time to see that the whole point of living was for myself. I felt my life was worthless. Nevertheless, any hope then was a hope that saved me. Although I felt like a coward back then to turn back on my notion of death, I think choosing to live takes a great deal of courage. For anyone who has contemplated death due to mental issues, know that the will to live requires a daring spirit to face life in all its challenges, especially if you're a deep, sensitive person. Finding the tenacity to live with the pain constantly felt, the overwhelming intense emotions, the depths of loneliness, the grave lack of misunderstandings from this world and that isolation of yourself in your own inner world of thoughts is an arduous and solitary journey. No one would or could have understood completely. But that's why these words provided relief. It becomes a form of alleviation and consolation that you're not alone, that the journey can take a different route and the world can be seen through a different lens.

What followed after that tiny voice that said, "I will save me," was that I decided to take responsibility for making myself happy again. It wasn't a straight route with precise steps and the change definitely took months and years of cultivation. It is still a journey in progress for me and I'm grateful to share that my anxiety attacks have reduced significantly. These days, I get a panic attack only when I'm in a tremendously stressful situation and even so, I'm able to manage it better. I manage my triggers and stress better before I reach a full-fledged attack. I can count the times I'm having chest pain in a year and even the notion of death is almost non-existent. I wouldn't say that I'm completely recovered but life now is hopeful, possible and meaningful. After trying and testing so many ways to reach my current state, here are some of the things that have worked for me. I've only listed things that I can still continuously find solace in to keep myself balanced. Other things that I've tried but have not remained consistent in practice will be included at the end.

1. Setting simple and small goals

Yes, it sounds simple but it really works. One contributor to my high-stress levels were the high expectations that I had imposed on myself. How I tend to set ridiculous goals for myself. Then stressing myself over them, and then chiding myself afterwards for not being able to complete them. It became a vicious cycle.

I built my self-confidence back again through setting extremely simple goals such as, wake up today and make my bed.

Take a 15 mins nature walk.

Do 3 mins of meditation.

Write one positive sentence about myself.

Knowing that I can accomplish these simple goals encourages and motivates me to have something to look forward to daily. As long as I complete one of these, I tell myself that I've done my best for the day and my life is worth living.

As someone who can't really adhere to repetitive goals, I have over time learned not to put a number to what I do. Example, I don't set goals such as 'I will journal daily' or to workout 4 times a week. Once I put a number to it and fail to do it, I get too discouraged and affected. This was the initial disappointment that I felt which put me back on an anxious scale. What worked for me is just having to do something that I'm accountable to myself for daily but it doesn't matter how many times I've done it in a week. As long as every day, I set a goal that makes me look forward to living a happy life. Today, it is to write my chapter on anxiety.

2. Meditation

I would be lying to say meditation is easy. It was tough for me. I started with 3 mins and found myself dozing off every time. Gradually, I could sit awake for 3 full minutes and I extended it to 5. Some days I miss it, sometimes for a week. It's a discipline in progress and its results are subtle and unconscious. It's the idea of compounding interest. You probably won't see an immediate reward but unconsciously, you would begin to see life through a calmer sort of lens. Today, I can sit for 10-30mins in stillness and silence. Some days I have more racing thoughts and I might feel like it's a lousy practice. This leads me to the next point.

3. Talking to myself

If only I could make myself happy, I could start to connect deeper with myself. I talk to myself in various ways. For example, if I had a lousy meditation practice and I started criticising myself for it, if I could catch it, I would talk to myself: "May, you are good. You are good enough. You sat down to meditate and that's good enough. I'm proud of you." If I can, I challenge as many of my self deprecating thoughts and replace them with kind and gentle affirmations. The other way that I communicate with myself is through journaling. Next point,

4. Journaling

Journaling has saved my life. I journal on paper, in books, on my phone, laptop, anywhere and everywhere. Especially when I feel intense emotions that I can't comprehend, I write them out. I get honest with how I feel, especially about the really nasty thoughts like I wish I could kill someone. I just get really honest. Get the disgusting nasty thoughts out. Sometimes we think it's bad to harbour such ideas and we suppress them. For me, I train myself to face the darkest most negative thoughts. And I write it all out. A reflection of how dark my inner nature is. And at the same time, witnessing this is me also allows me to be real me with me. Over time, allowing becomes accepting me for me. Miraculously with acceptance, these darker thoughts begin to subside. Once I've acknowledged my imperfections and shadows, I am then able to discover the light that is shining at it. As what Carl Jung has said, "One does not become enlightened by imagining figures of light, but by making the darkness conscious.".

5. Exercising

I find exercising extremely beneficial in improving my overall health. Its physical benefit is most obvious and so is its mental benefits. Whenever I get a good sweat going, my mind seems less cluttered. My body feels good and that naturally translates to improvements in my perception of self. As I'm a visual person, I visualise my stagnant and negative energy being released through my perspiration from a good workout. It doesn't always have to be dripping tonnes of sweat to be a good workout though. I had slipped discs at L4 and L5 for a period which hindered my ability to work out but it didn't stop me from taking long walks as a substitute. Every morning, even on the busiest ones, I commit to 5 minutes of stretching It's amazing how 5 minutes of a combination of touching toes, downward dogs and swirling my arms forwards and backwards help lift my morning mood. When I'm done with any form of stretch or workout, I always also say a nice thank you to my body. I give it a good squeeze from my feet, calves, to my body and arms. I hug myself and say, "Thank you body, I love you." This way, I work with my body and not against it. This way, I recognise myself, my effort to do something small for myself, my intentions. Besides, who else is there to cheer for me if I don't be my own greatest cheerleader? You are your own greatest ever cheerleader.

6. Nature

Taking walks and spending time in nature is one of the best gifts of life. It's free, it's accessible, it's abundant and the outcome is always positive. I love gazing at the clouds move swiftly through the skies, taking a walk through the park. I get lost looking at the leaves on the trees swaying. My favourite is being anywhere near water sources like the beach, a lake or a river. It is my time to space out, to think about nothing while staring at the vastness and to be recharged with positivity from Nature. If time is too scarce for an outdoor experience, bring nature into your environment. Have a plant that you need to take care of and be responsible for. When we tend to something delicate outside of ourselves, our focus is less on our lack but on giving our best. Start with something as simple as a cactus or an easy plant, and then build up. There were many times just taking a short outdoor walk at the park has lifted me from my waves of sadness and melancholy.

It is not that by doing all the above, anxiety will be gone. It still comes to me and I still have my triggers. But what's shared above has helped me to cope better when the internal Monster does visit. It has helped me to recognise my triggers better, to find ways that are working for me, to reduce my triggers rather than against me.

Some other things that I've also tried include, taking up dance classes, learning how to sing my favourite songs, signing up for workshops and talks on my subjects of interest, joining new interest groups to meet like-minded friends, yoga, going to a museum and cafe-hopping. These are the other things that I've tried inconsistently but have also helped me in my journey of coping better with anxiety. The key is to try out something that you enjoy, that makes you happy without an end goal. For example, I took up dancing but when I stopped finding time to go for it, I didn't beat myself up for stopping halfway. I've enjoyed it and I've also other commitments in place that help regulate my anxiety. No judgements for self and it is all but an experience.

About Maybelline Tan

Maybelline Tan, also known as That Wild Notebook on Instagram, is a passionate educator working with children, life coach and writer. In coaching, she works with youths and women to help them discover their authentic nature. That Wild Notebook is a reflection of Maybelline as an ordinary person living her life fully in presence. It represents her love for all things wild in nature and penning down her reflections in notebooks. Being a contemplator of nature and poetry, she often questions what is the meaning of life? For Maybelline, the meaning of life is to discover our essential nature, our authentic selves.

That Wild Notebook reveals the transition in Maybelline throughout her young adult years and contains various aspects of her 'self' that are still evolving. Most importantly, it is an identity for her to create her authentic expression. On the surface, it seems ordinary just like any other profiles and that is what it is. She is an ordinary person who knows the worth she possess within, and she is passionate about working with women and youths who feels ordinary but know they have a lot more to give. Maybelline loves to help others who are at a juncture looking for directions, someone with a fire burning within and seeking that source to ignite. She'd love to work with you in helping you to figure out your lighted path. Her specialities include: conscious living, women's issues, finding your purpose, troubled youths and being a Highly Sensitive Person (HSP).

You may reach her at tse.maybelline@gmail.com. View her ordinary musings on Instagram: @thatwildnotebook. Feel connected through her writings on Medium: Medium.com@thatwildnotebook. Check out her trial and errors from LinkedIn: Linkedin.com/in/maybelline-tan

The Irrationality Of Batman
by Mohd Hijazi

I still remember that fateful Thursday evening - the 14th of September 2017, the birthday of my two closest friends. I woke up from a nap at around 5 pm, all ready and primed for a soccer match happening later that night. The cold breeze that blew through the windows as I opened them, made me sniffle slightly. "Bad timing for a cold, Jaz" I thought to myself. I had just recovered from a bout of man flu and was really looking forward to a game of soccer to just get into the groove again. My wife looked at me and asked if I was still proceeding with my plan of playing, and I nodded enthusiastically. She sighed in resignation knowing that there was not much she could say to persuade me otherwise. I chuckled at her response.

The wall clock struck 7 pm and I made my way out of the house, decked in the colors of my team with my football attire in my sling bag. My friend was picking me up, and I proceeded to the meeting point and waited. I was still a few minutes early.

The air was still cold and it took me awhile to somehow realize that I was developing a bit of a muscle ache. The ache was developing around the back of my neck, and I felt terribly uncomfortable. Remembering that I had a bottle of heat salve somewhere in my kit I took it out, slapped a generous amount of the therapeutic cream on and rubbed it vigorously on the aching spot. I let out a huge sigh of relief which was evidently heard by my friend who arrived on the dot. "Are you okay?" he asked. I just smiled faintly, slightly puzzled by the onset of these niggling aches.

The pace of the soccer match was fast and furious. Our opponents that evening were a team of dynamic, fit and agile players who ran circles around us. I was getting more and more frustrated with every single minute that passed. We were struggling badly. I looked towards the side of the pitch for some much needed support. Understandably, only faces of bewilderment greeted me. Halfway through the match, my stamina ran out. I was literally walking around the field in a daze. The dejectedness and despondency I felt obviously showed. I could hear shouts and cries from my teammate asking me to look lively and contribute productively to the game. At that very moment, "the thing" happened.

What was "the thing" you ask? It was a moment I will not forget anytime soon.

I still remember it, and the way it unfolded on the field that night. Suddenly, a cold chill ran up my spine. I burped unexpectedly; a build-up of gas was forming. It stopped me in my tracks for a moment. It took all my effort to try to gain some semblance of control over my body. The feeling was absolutely alien to me. I began rubbing my stomach and chest trying to burp out the excess air. Bizarrely enough, I began feeling dizzy and a blanket of blurry blackness began to envelop my eyes. I placed my palm against my chest and felt a gradual increase in its thumping rate. It felt strange. I knew at that moment that I needed to get off the field.

I called out to the referee and signaled for a change. I tried jogging slowly to the sidelines. All I could sense was the energy draining down my legs. I lumbered clumsily, while calling out to a teammate to replace me. Even the voice that escaped my throat was a whimper. A barely noticeable squeak. As I walked slowly off-pitch, I sensed that my fingers were getting clammy. Beads of inexplicably cold sweat trickled down my forehead. Seating myself as comfortably as I could on the cold, hard stone steps, I tried reconciling myself with the situation. What was it? I kept asking myself. Why is my body shutting down like this? Some of my teammates, perhaps noticing the abrupt and significant change in my body language asked, if I was okay. I just waved them off apologetically, torn between offering an explanation and asking myself for that explanation.

My mind was racing through the various medical symptoms I had read about online, in a bid to rationalize what I was feeling physically. I tried walking it off to no avail. The cold air seemed to amplify the foreboding feeling of doom. Instinctively I searched my bag and grabbed my mobile phone. Something innate was telling me that I needed medical attention. I dialed 995. Taking whatever strength I could gather, I provided the necessary information to the responder on the other end of the phone line. As I put the phone down, many thoughts flooded my mind. Worry ensued. Fear gripped. Hopelessness beckoned.

The minutes that passed waiting for the ambulance felt like an eternity. I smiled wryly at each passing teammate that walked past. One by one they asked if everything was okay for me. Just as I was about to slump my weary body against the pillar, I saw the flickering bright lights of the arriving ambulance. The mixed feelings of relief and worry gained momentum. The responders rushed over to me, and asked the standard questions to assess the level of attention needed. The whole mood around me changed to that of concern. Verbal instructions were exchanged over me, like some clockwork machinery working on a scheduled dateline. The confused look on my face must have prompted the responder to quip, "Relax. You are feeling anxious." That part of me wanted to retaliate "How the hell am I supposed to relax when you are plugging things into me all over." They propped me up on the stretcher and pushed me quickly into the back of the ambulance. The level of worry increased when they started filling the syringe. "Am I going to be okay?" I asked. The responders looked at each other. "Yes, we just need to calm you down, as your heartbeat is just too fast. And that is not good."

The ride to the hospital was like journeying into an abyss of the vast unknown. I muttered whatever prayers I could, hoping and wishing that somehow I could get to hear the voice of my wife and my children. I began reflecting back on my life. Somehow that clichéd idea that our lives will flash before us upon impending death seemed to be happening in my awareness. I was feeling helpless and hopeful all at the same time. "Was this all my life, I thought? To wither and perish in the middle of a soccer match?"

It is anybody's guess what exactly transpired that night. But it changed me. In a way I never quite expected. The doctors' tests that night showed no anomalies. I was given muscle relaxants and a lot of assuring words to the effect that there was nothing physically wrong with me. X'rays were done the same night, followed by intensive rounds of CT scans and treadmill runs. I alternated from being in a state of being relaxed to having episodes of unexplained panic attacks. I had to call out to the nurses numerous times throughout the night.

In the morning, while on his ward rounds the doctor came over to me and said that I was perhaps experiencing atypical GERD symptoms. At the time I could not comprehend what GERD was all about. All I was preoccupied about was that insatiable all-consuming need to be home with my children. I later found out that GERD stands for Gastroesophageal Reflux Disease. It occurs when food and stomach acids back up from the stomach into the oesophagus.

The doctor gave me the all-clear to be discharged that same afternoon, with a set appointment in the coming months. It was strange to have been so gutted the night before while being assured that there was nothing conclusively worrying with me physically. Little did I realize that the damage done was more psychological.

In the ensuing weeks I descended into an intense turmoil. It was emotional and psychological and hugely unsettling. I felt something within me was fractured. The few weeks straight after my discharge were filled with gripping fears of death. I seemed to have developed an aversion towards being alone, even for a wee moment. There was a constant need to be around people, to put it mildly. When my wife and children left for school early in the morning, I insisted on taking the same cab with them, dropping them off and travelling onwards to my mother's place. And thus I stayed at my mother's place during the early half of each day, with the comforting assurance that someone would be around to care for me.

My career suffered. As a financial advisor, I was needed to make appointments constantly and meet with prospective clients at their convenience and availability. There were times when prospects would, as is the norm, request for an evening or late night appointment. I had to decline unwillingly. The irrational anxiety and fear of being out alone during the latter part of the day worried me. I declined a lot of speaking engagements and invitations to Toastmasters events. As a result of these adjustments to my normally active and action-filled life, I sensed that I was becoming more reclusive, socially.

Physically, the changes could not have been more drastic. From the very moment I was admitted into hospital to under a fortnight later, my weight dropped by a dramatic 22 kilograms. The weight loss worried me so much. From a soccer playing weight of around 70 kilograms, I became a scrawny 50 kilogram shadow of my former self. It was a massive shock to my loved ones not to mention myself. It was too sudden and too much. Not only that, I tired myself out far too easily. A walk down two flights of stairs made me breathless. My heart rate would spike to ridiculously high levels. What was all this, I thought to myself? I lost count of the number of times I dialed for an ambulance at night, just because a cup of coffee had made my heart start racing, and the panic that ensued had made me frantic. Yet when the responders came, all that was needed was just a calming presence and their words assuring me that all the panic and anxiety was in my head.

I was suffering. I just didn't know from what.

It was only in early 2018, that I chanced upon an article which a friend of mine, Carolyn had shared on her Facebook feed. Something about post traumatic syndrome disorder (PTSD). I casually clicked on it and read through the article. Understanding the article took me a while, but I began to see a light. The article gave insights on the symptoms and signs of the disorder. I was gobsmacked to say the least. It described in totality every single one of the physical and mental manifestations I had encountered over the past few months. The article gave so much information that I had to dive right into its inner sanctums. I spent the next few months extensively and intensively searching and reading up on anything remotely precious towards my understanding of the disorder. I knew that much of my recovery would depend on me knowing what i was up against.

After months of reading up, watching videos and listening to podcasts on the subject, I became acquainted with two very important terms. "Triggers" and "Coping Mechanisms". I realized that somehow "the thing" that had happened on that fateful September night had triggered a primal fear in me. It was a fear so irrational yet powerful enough to evoke the damning physical manifestations in my body. Even certain keywords, smells and places were able to rekindle and ignite that foreboding sense of anxiety and doom in me. I remembered how, even during that period of voracious reading and learning about the disorders, there were instances when I would have to get off the train I was riding on, breathing heavily, body slumped against walls or railings, just because I had been certain that a cardiac arrest, leading to my death in the train, was inevitable.

Amidst the darkness of learning what to do when the anxiety attacks would prevail over common sense, I managed to discover by chance some coping mechanisms that were helpful. A bottle of water, became my metaphorical life buoy. The bottle of water became a symbolic lifesaver, when I would feel my eyes suddenly going blurry, racing heartbeats or heavy breathing. There were instances when I had to redirect my taxi rides to the nearest shop or petrol kiosk, just so that I could grab a life-saving bottle of mineral water. Taxi drivers would just start to panic at my insistences and quietly assist. I figured that it was perhaps easier to listen and follow instructions than to lift an immobile, panic stricken passenger off the back seat.

Over the past three years, I have learned how to better manage my anxieties and these episodes when PTSD is triggered. It boiled down mostly to learning how to regain control of my mind's driver's seat. There were mornings and nights, when I would just be brought back to that fateful September night. The memory instantaneously triggered an avalanche of dread. I would start perspiring, feeling visually cramped and the heart racing and racing. It would then take me that much needed amount of will and strength to just calm my mind down by erasing or replacing the alarming visuals playing in my awareness with new, more calming and assuring ones. I later discovered that this was a form of the 'swish' technique, from NLP (NeuroLinguistic Programming). I had to learn how to moderate my breathing and liberate my fears and worries. Among other things, I learned to let go and submit to that irrationality at times.

More than anything, I believe that the key to my newfound ability to alleviate my anxieties was about understanding and learning the right knowledge. If I had not stumbled upon the shared article by my friend, I would have still been languishing in total ignorance of my disorder. Knowing what was happening and formulating the right and effective coping and healing strategies was crucial.

I used to think dismissively about people with anxieties and disorders like PTSD. I was convinced that they just lacked the willpower and positivity required to gain control of their thoughts and emotions. Having gone through the worst parts of the ordeal, and still finding ways of coping my way to recovery, I have discovered that there is so much more support that is needed in this field of study.

Anxiety, as I learned, was not just about what is happening within us. It is also about what is happening to us.

I've always fashioned myself to be as fearless as my iconic comic hero, Batman. This ordeal made me realize that the only part that made Batman human, was that sense of irrational fear within him. And for all I know, even Batman is still struggling with it still. If this is what makes me more of a human, then so be it.

About Mohd Hijazi

Hijazi is a passionate and vociferous individual when it comes to self development and empowerment. He speaks dynamically on the subjects of leadership and influence, salesmanship and effective engagement.

He has an innate interest in coaching and mentoring individuals on creating powerful and engaging personalities to enhance their personal and professional lives. Hijazi believes in the philosophy that communication and influence are key factors of success. He aspires to share insights that will provide you with a framework to excel at both.

In June 2014, Hijazi founded Success Guild, as a training platform, for him to conduct his signature self development programs. He hopes to build, link and empower a community of confident and competent mavericks via Success Guild.

To find out more about Hijazi and Success Guild, please visit SuccessGuild.org

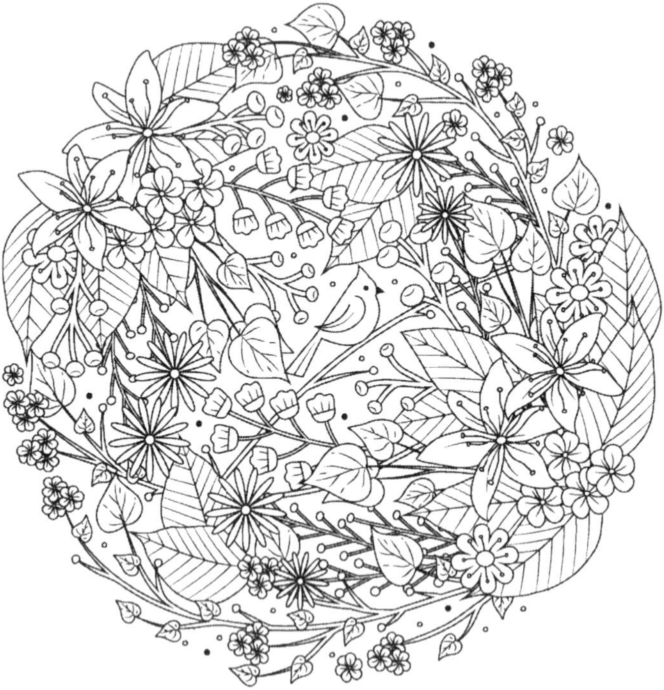

Dealing With Anxiety To ToastMasters
by Stephanie Fam

For someone who was born with a very obvious physical disability I come with a juicy, spiky sense of often dark humour. Let me describe myself to you: I have tentacle-like arms, snake-like fingers and flamingo-like legs and a bony bum that sticks to my wheelchair - more precisely a pushchair as it has to be pushed - like a Formula 1 racing driver adheres to his Ferrari while zooming round the bends at the annual Night Races. Comments like "You're so brave" and "You're so strong to be able to live like this!" trip off the tongues of my fans and foes alike. While I often don't have the heart to dispel these notions, the truth is that even the strongest and bravest of us experience some level of anxiety in our daily lives - making me no exception…

Contrary to popular belief it is not merely the lack of mobility that causes me anxiety but the concoction of effects due to my disability. Said disability is known these days as Quadriplegic Cerebral Palsy or the affectionately abridged quad CP. Quad as it affects all four of my limbs. Movement is jerky rather than spastic per se. Those who know me prefer 'jazzy'. For the purposes of this chapter I will focus on two types of anxiety: Body Dysmorphic Anxiety (anxiety due to shame or distaste towards ones own body) and Performance Anxiety. Judging by the way I jokingly described my physicality right at the beginning, readers are likely to assume that I harbour no sort of anxiety towards my physicality. Truth be told, there were periods in my teen and adolescent years where I really struggled to look at myself in the mirror! Every time, all the time.

When I was put in situations where I had to face a mirror, it seemed as if my brain was constantly on the run but could never find a place to hide! With all that said, how did the once shy, quiet and reserved teenager who could barely face her own reflection, blossom into a woman who now faces audiences as part of her work as a public speaker and emerging theatre-maker?

Honestly I didn't actively go off in search of a way to cope with my body dysmorphic anxiety. In fact as with most things that happen with me, life puts me where I least expect it to. I have often heard the phrase "To fully overcome a challenge, one must face it head on" by Anon. Little did I know how much the phrase would ring true for me when I stumbled upon what I thought was a 'workshop' that turned out to be a Toastmasters demonstration meeting. For readers who are unfamiliar with the worldwide movement, Toastmasters International is a public speaking platform where people of all walks of life can discover, improve or enhance their Speaking, Communication and Leadership skills. This is achieved through delivery of a series of speeches, skill-centred presentations and designated tasks at the preferred pace of each individual member. One then receives feedback from their peers going through the same process.

So how *did* Toastmasters help me cope with my self-directed anxiety? (Wait, doesn't facing a crowd of people cause me anxiety too?) It was where I unearthed my innate flair as a speaker, bringing my focus to what I wanted people to hear and not what I thought I looked like or how audiences viewed my physicality. A perfect example of this would be my maiden Toastmasters speech. I furiously prepared and practiced that lone speech for 3 weeks before the afternoon's meeting in which I was due to deliver it to an audience comprising living, breathing humans.

One would think that with the 3 weeks of relentlessly intense planning, preening and preparation that the speech went off without a hitch. Far from it. Instead, the minute I was wheeled onto the speaking area and uttered the first few words of my speech, I became acutely aware of the expectant faces, their many eyes on me. My brain was thrown into overdrive with thoughts such as "Oh my God…Too many eyes… Make them stop staring at me… Please!" The overload of thought soon translated into a physical reaction (accurately described as spasms which involve uncontrollable and involuntary arm or leg movements) making me feel as if I would blackout at any moment. Just as I was about to reach the end of my rope, I realized that if I gave in to my anxiety, then all I have worked hard up to this point would go to waste. Deciding to push past the mental and physical overload, I powered on through the remainder of the speech, keeping focus on what I wanted to relay to the audience. This obviously did the trick because I ultimately won my very first Best Speaker ribbon!

The Toastmasters movement has not only been a space that has helped me develop as a speaker and leader, but it is also a place where I forged what I consider to be one of the most significant and treasured bonds in life. It is the bond I share with the one and only Cookie (most unsporting of her to not allow me to reveal her real identity). If there was any doubt that the presence of a friend and loved one can alleviate an individual's anxiety, (at least for me) Cookie dispels that. One particular instance which clearly shows what I just mentioned happened when I was a guest speaker at one of the many Toastmaster Clubs in Singapore. Having delivered my speech I was expecting to receive an evaluation of it as was the norm for any Toastmaster meeting. Stepping up into the designated speaking area, my randomly chosen evaluator started off by saying "That was really an inspiring speech… but I believe Cerebral Palsy is caused by some genetic dysfunction in your family bloodline yes?" The minute the words left her mouth I think I could only choke out a hoarse "No" before realizing Cookie was already urging my gobsmacked evaluator to "get a move on", knowing how such a misinformed observation was going to affect me emotionally.

By this time, I was gripping Cookie's hand (clinging on for support if I were being honest) because I never felt more insulted and humiliated than I did right at that moment! My brain was screaming for me to "GET OUT OF THERE NOW " Maybe it was due to the inexplicable strength of our bond which I can't explain because Cookie read my mind and asked if I wanted to leave the room, which I wholeheartedly agreed to. Once outside,

I released all I had been feeling since that misinformed observation was made in the form of tears, Cookie holding me while I sobbed wailed and screamed at the horror and sheer repugnance of it all.

Besides being a physical presence in alleviating my various anxieties, Cookie has handed down her knowledge of alternative healing modalities in a bid to help me cope with my anxiety. What I particularly like to use to calm myself down in the midst of a sticky situation (when I cannot have Cookie close by) come in the form of clearing statements. These are primarily used in a modality known as Access Consciousness® such as "What else is possible? "What's good about this that I'm not getting?" "Who does that belong to" and "How does it get any better than this? These statements come in especially handy with my theatre work where my brain has to adapt to by the minute changes in quick succession. An example of this was when I had to rewrite an entire script within 48 hours!

So far, I've touched on specific methods (and a very important person) that help me cope with anxiety. However, I realize I almost forgot to mention my favourite forms of anxiety-release… Poetry-writing and Abstract Line Drawing.

Such artistic mediums act as blank canvases for me to express myself without restriction, in a way allowing me to let go of what I would otherwise keep hidden.

Coping with anxiety of any kind is an ever-challenging road that constantly evolves. I do not think there will ever be a direct "cure" but as long as we have the tools to deal with it and use them as best as we can, we're doing the best thing possible!

About Stephanie Fam

Public speaker, trained hypnotist, energy healing professional and multi-disciplinary artist, Stephanie views life as an ever–evolving landscape where one has to always be open to new ways of navigation. From a similar standpoint, Stephanie feels that in coping with anxiety, one needs to be given the freedom to discover and test which methods work best for them. Methods such as hypnotherapy, energy work, fresh air, access bars and the access clearings, emotional freedom technique, poetry-writing, abstract line drawing and listening to your favourite music.

Her decade-long experience on the public speaking platform of Toastmasters International allows her to encourage, motivate and inspire live audiences through meticulously crafted speeches. Through her portfolio, she strives to be a voice advocating for disability-led practices within the artistic community.

The Anxiety Mindset
by Didi Kan

Anxiety is the feeling of fear in the body. Anxiety is the voice of the child inside of us, constantly reminding us that we have been hurt in the past and we may get hurt again.

The child's mind and the adult's mind
The mind is divided in 2 distinct parts. The subconscious mind and the conscious mind. I call them respectively the child's mind and the adult's mind. They can work separately or together in various ratio of percentage and power.

The child's mind is an emotional mind. The child feels. The child is also the bookkeeper as it remembers all the informations we have downloaded from our formative years. All those datas and memories form our program, our subconscious automatic pilot, our Sat Nav. And because the child's mind is an emotional mind all those informations are stored into a raw emotional format.

The adult's mind on the other hand is logical, creative and organisational. Every time we take decisions and when we use rationale, analytical, deduction, intelligence and the coordination of our imagination we operate our adult's mind.

Whenever we feel overwhelmed by emotions however it is a sign that the child's mind has taken over.

We are who we believe we are

When we are children we are at a developmental and non judgemental stage. We absorb the reality and the truth of our surroundings and the adults around us. We shape our sense of worth and identity on our observations, experiences and what people we look up to tell us about ourselves.

Our sense of worth and identity dictates the course of our existence, as it not only determines who we think we are in the world, but it is also directly and symbiotically related to what we think is available to us or not, based on our perceived abilities and limitations.

Example 1: We have been called "stupid" repetitively during childhood by a parent or a teacher, we end up believing we are stupid. We come to the conclusion that succeeding at intellectual tasks is not available to us. Which implies that exposing ourselves to intellectual tasks equates exposing ourselves to the risk of failure and rejection. Because we are hardwired to belong to our tribe, rejection is terrifying. As a result the child's mind always remembers we may suffer rejection, and triggers anxiety every time, as adult, we are facing the prospect of a challenge that involves intelligence.

Example 2: We witness our parents struggle with money. We associate money with struggle, unhappiness, absence, stress, arguments and illnesses perhaps. As a result we believe that money is toxic. Which develops into the belief that safe, happy and benevolent money is not available to us. That creates a money blockage that hinders our capacity at generating prosperity without toxic side effects. And the vision we have of ourselves is of someone that can never enjoy abundance fully and freely. We may be able to attract money, but at the cost of our health, happiness, sacrifices, anxiety, and the majority of our precious time, just like for our parents.

Example 3: We have been put on the spot and humiliated by a teacher in front of the whole class. As we freeze in terror of the impending rejection sentence, we interpret that ordeal like a public trial, a judgement. We believe that we don't fit the standards of that society. We conclude subsequently that being safe from the risk of being under scrutiny again is not available to us and we may suffer deadly consequences. The stress experienced creates a strong survival association, that triggers the same feelings felt on that day, each time we face a group of people staring at us again. That often develops into a fear of public speaking, and potentially social anxiety.

As we grow into adulthood the child's voice becomes our narrative. The voice in our head and the stories we tell ourselves are no more no less than the child inside of us, constantly reminding us who we are and our role and limitations in the world.

And here is the problem: We navigate through life with our adult's mind, thinking that we are in charge, unbeknown to the fact that the conscious mind is only 5% of our mind, and that we are actually under the hold of the mighty (95%) subconscious and emotional child's mind. A mind that has never been designed or updated to support an adult's life. We essentially live our adult life using an outdated and reactive emotional mind.

Knowing is the realm of the adult's mind and believing is the realm of the child's mind. Whatever the adult knows, is worth little until and unless the child believes it too. So if the child believes certain things are not available, no matter how much we know they should be, the child will sabotage our attempts at trying to get these things, and the failure at getting these things confirms our sense of worth and identity.

Coping mechanism

The fundamental reason as to why people suffer from anxiety is because they own a poor coping mechanism. We all get exposed to various types of fears and stresses all throughout our life. It was never about the fears or the stresses. It is about how WE regulate them or not. And that ability or inability at regulating fears and stresses is inherited.

It is important to highlight that children learn more by observing information than being taught information. So if parents tell them something but don't behave accordingly, children will copy their behaviours, not their words.

So if a child witnesses violence, arguments or abuse at home, the child will learn from the adults that in the face of adversity there is no way to regulate stress for the members of its tribe, and that it is the way they act, interact with and react to people. The child downloads the parents beliefs. The belief that the only choice they have when confronted to fear and stress is to loose control. Because the power of deescalating and neutralising a situation is not available to them.

If the child suffers violence or abuse directly, the impact is amplified hundredfolds.

Fear is an illusion

Since anxiety is the feeling of fear in the body we must understand fear. Fear is a signal. The original survival tool. The cue telling us that we are going to face the unknown again. Our attitude towards fear is the reflection of the behaviours we have observed and borrowed from our tribe (parents, education, culture, religion, society).

If our parents and mentors demonstrate all the ropes of a solid coping mechanism (stress regulator) and exhibit all the attributes of a dynamic growth mindset (curiosity, humility, acceptance and open mindedness to change and adaptation) we grow into their model and there is nothing that life can throw at us that we can't survive, adapt to and grow from. For the rest and the majority of us, antediluvian tribal cycles, that are essentially obsolete beliefs passed over generationally, will infect us with the assumption that what is in the unknown might harm us. And we fear the unknown. And fear becomes an over zealous protection mechanism.

So fear was never the problem. The problem is our relationship with the unknown. The not knowing wether "we will survive the next time" or not. We forget that the unknown was never anything for us to fear, as all the things that matter the most to us we learn them from what was once the unknown. The unknown is knowledge, freedom and infinite possibilities. The unknown is what exists outside the walls of our comfort zone. Outside the gates of our golden prison. And it is in that very same unknown that lie all the things we want and the keys for us to get them.

The only reason we allow fear to exist and persist in our life is because we believe that fear is somehow useful to us. We are only born with two fears: the fear of falling and the fear of loud noises. All other fears are acquired and mimicked from our tribe. And although fear may help create and reinforce some associations that serve us, we don't need fear. If for instance I have been scalded by boiling water in the past, it is not the fear from being burnt again that prevents me from putting my hand in the boiling water. It is my intelligence. Reminding me of the lesson I have learnt from that experience. The rise of intelligence made fear redundant.

As with all rules are exceptions. Fear can be real and useful in rare and extreme contexts. For the vast majority of those living in a developed country not at war, and for the vast majority of our life 99.99% of our fears are illusions and utterly obsolete to our well being and development, as they are only speculations and extrapolations of past hurts projected into the future.

Anxiety only exists when our mind is in the future

Because it wants to protect us, the child's mind keeps on roaming through time, being constantly angry at the past and scared of the future, in a bid to keep us reminded, alert and ready against any possible harm.

Paradoxically and ironically, when we allow our mind to wander back and forth into the past and the future we are at our most disempowered state, because there is nothing we can do there. We can only take an action now. We can only create change now. And that inability to influence an event remind us of how powerless and defenceless we felt as a child, reinforces learnt helplessness, and generates anxiety.

It is important to reiterate that since 95% of our thoughts are subconscious, we are often under the emotional influence of the child, even though we are performing a task under the supervision of the adult's mind. When we execute activities we are so familiar with that they don't require our full attention (fast mode), enough of the mind can travel through time and trigger anxiety. The level of focus we use at any given time is therefore directly proportionally related to how much grounds we are allowing for anxiety to spread and be felt in our body in that moment.

We get addicted to our feelings

One of my specialism is addiction and we can look at anxiety from that perspective too. We often think of classical addictions such as smoking, alcohol, recreational drugs, prescription drugs, vaping, gambling, gaming, shopping, shoplifting, sex, porn, social media, working, exercising, sugar, crisps, chocolate, junk food... But we also get addicted to anger, anxiety, depression, self sabotage, self harm, stress, worries, acceptance, praises, dramas, therapy, competing, comparing, insecurity, power, status, over thinking, self negative talk, control, toxic people, co dependency, narcissists, nostalgia... We can and we do get addicted to anything. Because we don't get addicted to the things we do. We get addicted to how we feel when we do these things. We get addicted to the feelings. To our own internal bio chemistry.

We are creatures of feelings. We need to feel to know that we exist. And although anxiety is a terribly unpleasant feeling, if our most familiar feelings are various levels of fears and anxiety, we will get high on the peaks of Cortisol. Cortisol being a highly addictive hormone produced in the body by stress. And that augments the difficulty for many anxiety sufferers to even seek help because the mind wants this, and will often sabotage our conscious attempts at getting better.

We get addicted to our comfort zone

We are creatures of habit. The mind loves what feels familiar, regardless of wether it serves our well being or not. It is the only way it understands survival. So if we have been suffering from anxiety for a long time (and that is also true for all mental and emotional imbalances) and we are still alive, anxiety is perceived as familiar, and even homely. An insidious and cruel normality that offers no solace, respite or alternatives, and yet feels paradoxically safe from the brain's standpoint.

Imprints ==> Belief System ==> Narrative ==> Habits of thoughts ==> Habits of feelings and emotions ==> Habits of Actions ==> Our life ==> The reality we keep on allowing and repeating.

Anxiety is a habit, and all we need to do to free ourselves from that habit is to replace it with a better, constructive and empowering new habit. Infinite myriads of parameters expand infinitely the rates of success with any method. And that is why I offer bespoke and specific services in my practice in London, to optimise the odds of a full and complete transformation. I do believe nevertheless that the protocol I am suggesting next has the potential to help many find clarity and kickstart their journey to recovery.

Reset

We must first slow down that train of thoughts of ours, that is constantly rushing into the future, leaving a trail of anxiety behind for us to suffer. Every time you feel anxiety starting to creep up in your body, create an emergency alarm signal and see the word PAUSE, written in big capital red neon letters, flashing right in front of your eyes. Then pause.

Use the grounding technique straight away:
- Name out loud 5 things you can see in your close proximity. Take the time to fully process each thing.
- Name out loud 4 things you can hear. Take the time to dissociate each sound.
- Touch 3 different textures and name them out loud. Take the time to fully feel them.

- Smell 2 different smells. Take the time to recognise each smell.
- Take 1 deep breath. As you inhale squeeze your fists and as many muscles in your body as you can. As you exhale open up your fists, release all muscles and say out loud:" LET GO".

Immediately run a body scan:" Do I feel any sharp pain in my body right now ? Am I burning ? Am I freezing ? Am I drowning ? NO". Then do an environmental scan:" Is there anything I should feel anxious about right here right now ? Is there a wild animal or a burglar about to attack me ? Are there imminent and real threats in this room ? NO".

Next dissociate yourself from the anxiety. Write the reason of the anxiety on a piece of paper. Then ask yourself:" That thing I was going to feel anxious about, can I do something to solve it now ?" If yes, take the appropriate action. If not, fold the piece of paper and put it in the freezer, a jar, a box or in your pocket, and move on with your thoughts. If you don't know what creates the anxiety write on the piece of paper:" feeling of anxiety".

Reveal

Next, and very quickly, grab the helm of the adult's mind fully by either (A) being mindful at what you do, (B) being mindful at what you observe, (C) being mindful at being grateful, (D) being mindful at teaching the child new, constructive and empowering beliefs, or (E) being mindful of the breath.

(A) We all understand how to be mindful at what we do because we use that skill regularly. Every time we are doing something important or new we recruit the whole of our adult's mind. And that is why we never feel anxious in those instances. That also explains why some people find hobbies like painting or puzzles calming and therapeutic. And why so many turn workaholic or develop other types of addiction. A 100% laser mind focus relieves us from anxiety momentarily since it leaves no room for it. As we enjoy solace from anxiety we associate the action or the distraction as the source of the relief. And as we return to that action or distraction repetitively to experience respite from anxiety again, this develops inexorably into an addiction. The addiction has become our coping mechanism.

We want to master our aptitude at being mindful at the things we do to not only free ourselves from the grip of anxiety, but also to optimise the very things we do. But we must raise the awareness that that skill is transferable to all of our actions, so not to create exclusive associations that lead to addiction.

Since whatever we focus our mind on we feel more in our body, and whatever we feel more in our body we create, allow and attract more in our life, it is also paramount to direct our focus solely on what we want and can, as opposed to what we don't want or can't. By doing so we send a command to the subconscious mind to work for us, like a secret heat seeking drone, to go seek, find and reveal our true potential.

(B) Mindfulness is observing the awareness of our thoughts and feelings about things, events, people and self without judgement. Without questioning, analysing or comparing. Without the labels the child has attached onto them. Just accepting that everything can be left in space and time, exactly where they are.

Thoughts and feelings are ephemeral by nature and are not meant to be kept hostage in our mind and body. They turn sterile at best and toxic at worst when trapped inside of us. They are meant to be experienced in the moment, and then freed up so we can experience new ones, and keep synchronised with the ever changing nature of the Universe. And we are totally free to choose the following ones as they just pass and go. We only hijack and recycle disempowering thoughts and feelings out of bad habits. Habits stemmed from the belief that it is normal to suffer fear and aggression on various levels of amplitude, intensity and context, because everyone around us share that same reality. So we just allow for fear and aggression to prevail and limit our life.

Letting go of the pernicious habits of fear and aggression reveals the truth that we are safe, happy and whole... that everything is perfect as it is, right here and right now.

Benches in public parks on a nice day are simple and easy places to start practicing mindfulness. We belong to nature. We were never meant to blossom in concrete, pollution, urban noises, deadlines, competitiveness, overcrowded public transportations, computer screens, tablets screens, mobile phones screens... Immersing ourselves in our natural habitat, merging with trees, plants, flowers, grass, sun, wind, birdsongs and bees offers a more intuitive and instinctive setting for us to learn and let go of all the noise from inside of our head. Once we master mind clarity we can bring that skill onto the battlefields and be stress and anxiety proof anywhere and anytime.

(C) The practice of gratitude is the art of conditioning our mind to look at the places that make us FEEL better, as opposed to keep on staring at all the places that make us FEEL worse. At a biological level practicing gratitude releases DHEA in the body, a happy, healing and feel good hormone that counteracts Cortisol (the stress hormone).

So if for instance I am queuing to see a show and the queue hasn't moved in 20 minutes, I can either stare at the front of the queue and fuel my frustration, or I can look at the back of the queue and realise that the queue behind me is now twice as long as the queue in front of me, and feel better straight away, without having moved an inch.

Gratitude is a magic filter we were all born with. Gratitude reminds us that there is always a better and a worse side, and we can choose at any moment to feel better just by looking in the right direction.

Relearn

(D) All children believe that some things are not available to them. The untaught truth is that EVERYTHING is available to any all of us. The only reason we haven't got some of the things we want in our adult's our life is because the child inside of us still believes that those things are unobtainable. Of course if I am born without legs, running a marathon may not be feasible to me. Finding worth, elation, success and purpose through the pursuit of a Paralympic discipline however is absolutely available to me.

Understanding and accepting that everything is available to us is the ultimate mindset to unlock our full potential. The key to free the secret truth about people. The truth that we are enough. And that we can be whatever and whoever we want to be. There is not a single quality or attribute we can't own, cultivate and excel at if we desire so, because we were born complete, with the infinite power to change, recalibrate, adapt and grow. We have just been taught to forget about it and to look in all the wrong places.

We must show the child that although it is true that some things were not available to us back then, because we were only a confused child in an adults world, things have changed. We are now powerful, independent and experienced adults ourselves. And all we ever need to do when we feel disempowered, hurt or confused is to switch on that adult's mind, and give that child a big hug. Because it is the adult that protects, comforts and praises the child. We must remind the child that everything is ok. We are safe. We are fine. We have got this. Because we are the adult, and it is the adult who takes charge, finds solutions and solves problems.

Reconnect

(E) Breathing is the most vital of our functions. The one action we sustain wether we are awake or asleep. Breathing slowly and mindfully resets the autonomous nervous system, raises our immune response and is the most simple, humble, yet efficient method to keep anxiety at bay, once we have anchored our mind back into the present. It matters not which tempo we are breathing at as long as we focus our attention on it, and we gradually and naturally allow for the breath to slow down, stabilise and unite with the moment.

Try this when you feel anxious: Breathe in for the count of 4 to 7, then hold the breath for the count of 4 to 7, then breathe out for the count of 4 to 7. Repeat 10 times and feel your autonomous nervous system resetting itself gradually. Once the anxiety is gone there is no longer any need to hold the breath. Just be mindful of the breathing flow...

Breathing also brings particles and atoms from the outside in our body. Breathing mindfully therefore reconciles us with the Universe. It reminds us that we were always safe, protected and supported by the Universe. Because oxygen is the primordial element for us to stay alive, and it comes from the outside.

Once the breath is back, a simple hack to prevent us from succumbing to fear again (and since our thoughts are a series of questions and answers) is to ask ourselves better questions (in order to bring out better answers). So when we think:" What will happen if I have a panic attack again and it doesn't work then ?". The answer is inevitably:" You may not survive". Choose instead:" How can I make sure I beat the anxiety 100% ?". The answer will be:" Keep at it. Repeat the full protocol, as many times as required and until it becomes a new natural habit...". And as we feel empowered being proactive at focusing on what we want, as opposed to what we don't want, as we are reinforcing new neural pathways in our brain corresponding to the new actions we are taking, we gradually and steadily learn to replace anxiety with a methodic and solid coping mechanism that allows us to reconnect to our full potential.

Faith is the opposite of fear

Life is made of time, so as long as we are alive time never stops. We own the choice each moment to either focus on sending a positive intent, worrying about future outcomes, or being disappointed by the outcomes of previous intents. An outcome is only the result of past intents, so they happen anyway in due time all through our life. Sending positive intents is like spreading seeds. Focusing on outcomes is like staring at the crops growing and expecting they will turn all right. Being angry or disappointed at outcomes is ignoring the rest of the immense field. The more we stare at the crops and the more we are disappointed by them, the more resistance we create, the less seeds we spread, and the less we make out of our time and potential.

Ultimately, focusing on intents all the time is fostering faith in ourselves. Faith in our ability to cope, recalibrate and adapt. Faith in our capacity to survive, live and thrive. Faith in the Universe... And because love is the opposite of fear and faith is the ultimate expression of love, faith is also the ultimate antidote against fear and anxiety.

The bigger picture
The Universe is everything in space and time. In the Universe there is no good or bad. Only polarities that create life and movements. For electricity to exist there needs to be a positive and a negative. The negative is not "bad". For weather fluctuations to happen in the sky there needs to be hot and cold. For a baby to be conceived there needs to be a man and a woman.

Neither opposite is intrinsically good or bad, or more or less important than the other.

The Universe is chaos. The Universe does not judge. We judge. And we must stop judging. Because judging diminishes our field of vision and possibilities. We must accept that there is nothing wrong about ourselves or the world. There are only experiences. And wether we believe the experiences are lessons or curses is down to the choice of mindset we own. We can be the adult, with the power of creating. Or we can be the child, who never had a choice to be anything else but a victim back then. We can choose to own, grow and use a Creator's mindset. Or we can choose to stay scared and angry and be owned by a Victim's mindset.

A Creator seeks growth in all experiences. A Creator always asks:" Why is this happening FOR me ?" And their subconscious mind, like a heat seeking drone will go, seek and find why this is happening FOR them. And this is how we continuously learn and grow from everything, and create a life of unlimited abundance.

A Victim on the other hand blames others for their misfortunes. Saying:" Why is it happening TO me !?". And the child's mind reminds them:" Because you were born to suffer injustice, because it is the way it is and there is nothing you can do about it". And we never learn from the experience.

The Universe always gives us whatever it knows is best for us. We can learn and grow from those lessons. Or repeat them over and over again, until and if we learn from them.

We are all the same

We all own the same value and potential. We all aspire for the same things. We want to be loved, happy, healthy and abundant. And we will all be exposed to the full spectrum of thoughts, feelings and emotions in our lifetime. They may manifest in different size, shape and configuration, at different times of our life and for different reasons, but we will all feel fear, love, happiness, sadness, forgiveness, anger... one way or another.

We will all experience success, rejection, highs and lows, injustice, prejudice and discrimination... from both sides. And we must understand that as long as we don't spend our life suffering, all "negative" and disempowering experiences are crucial to our humanity, as they teach us contrasts, relativity and empathy.

And because the Universe enjoys a paradox, once we have reached a greater level of consciousness something very special and precious happens. The hurt from the past converts into a higher level of appreciation, value and gratitude towards life.

Our best is good enough

Doing our best is all we want to do, because it is the best we can do. So as long as we do our best we can never be dissatisfied. But we must do our best each moment.

As Alan Watts said once:" life is not a journey, life is a dance, life is a song, we must enjoy each step and each note..." So we must do our best to enjoy doing our best each moment. Enjoy the process of recovering from the past and discovering and revealing a better new self, one day at a time. And as we do our best to enjoy doing our best, each moment, we don't need to wish or hope for things to get better in the future anymore, as they already are better in the moment. Our best is good enough, one moment, one breath and one positive intent at a time.

About Didi Kan

Didi Kan is an ex-alcoholic, class A drug addict, suicidal manic depressive of 25 years. He has used his extensive experience to develop a protocol that he is now using as a transformational therapist and coach specialised in anxiety, depression, addiction and self sabotage.

Didi is obsessed with the mechanics of the mind and how to optimise all aspects of our lives from that perspective and you are invited to follow his journey on social media for further content and updates about his upcoming books. All details are on his website: didikantransformation.com

The Gift Of Anxiety
by Hayley Amanda Hammer

It was a December morning in 2010 and I had been out the night before to a lavish American/Italian restaurant for dinner and drinks with a dear friend. We had so much fun that I didn't want the night to end!

So here I was, the morning after, in my car, driving to a job I didn't enjoy and wondering how I could get out of this arrangement. The woman I worked with, reminded me so much of my mum, she really didn't like herself and would take her angst out on me!

It was no coincidence that I met her at a life changing seminar. She approached me during the lunch break and said she sensed my energy would be a great contribution to her business. At that time, I was easily impressed if anyone thought I would be good for their life let alone their business! I was brought up to always put other peoples' needs first and to value their opinion. I should also mention that I had a mother who was not very loving or affectionate and would never approve of anything I did. This left me feeling inadequate and always seeking validation from others.

A month into working was enough for me to become aware that this was not what I was desiring in my life. When I first started on my transformational journey 25 years ago, I had no idea that what would show up today, would become an intrinsic part of the changes I had been asking for. You see, change doesn't always show up the way you think it does and it's not always comfortable!

Growing up was pretty tough, my relationship with my mum was turbulent, I never knew from one day to the next if she would be happy or mad about something, and all the while, I deeply yearned for her love. In 2003, she was diagnosed with ovarian cancer. I was devastated, I had spent many years healing our relationship and the next 12 months would prove to be sheer hell, as I watched her slowly deteriorate. I threw myself into studying every self-help book available and was aware that it was possible for her to change the cancer. I even went to see a friend who was into alternative therapy, to see if she had any ideas. She told me about a powerful energy healing technique known as Reiki. I had no idea what this was, or that it would lead me onto greater things, although I was curious to know more.

Over the course of 18 months, I was introduced to the world of energy healing and how it could treat many conditions. I committed to learning this incredible technique and to eventually become a Reiki master. Every class opened more awareness and after completing level 2, I suggested a course of treatments to my mum. She made it clear that she had no interest in what I had to offer and preferred to rely on the more traditional methods of chemotherapy. I started to realise how dependent I had become on her and my need to keep her alive, but I also knew deep down that she did not wish to continue living and so I asked my Reiki teacher if she would help me to let her go and to honour her choice.

After my mum passed away, I went through an intense phase of confusion, not knowing what I wanted to do or where I was heading. I felt so vulnerable and alone and the idea of not having her around made it harder for me to get on with my life. I had never made my own decisions, I had always relied on my mum to know what was best for me, as I hadn't done a very good job and according to her, I was prone to always making mistakes! It was time for me to live my own life and to trust I would always be okay. I had to learn to love and take care of myself, which was no easy task, as I had never been shown how to do this. One of my favourite books at the time was 'You can Heal Your Life' by Louise L. Hay. I would read it like it was my bible. It was the only thing I had to comfort me.

I especially loved the section at the back of the book where you could refer to a list of symptoms, that would give a description of the suggested thoughts or feelings that were creating it, with a daily affirmation to begin to change it. I also enjoyed reading Louise's biography, as I could really relate to it, and if she could turn her life around, then so could I!

When I looked up cancer, it suggested a lot of anger and resentment towards life. This was the case for my mum, and I knew there were a lot of things I was holding onto from the past that I felt needed to change. I continued to practice Reiki with a group of friends once a month and I began to have clients who were desperately seeking to change their life and their symptoms. After a short period of time, I became curious to know what really created illness and disease in our bodies and how we could change it.

It was in 2006 when I received an email that would completely change my life! It was an invitation to discover a dynamic body of work, known as Access Consciousness, that could clear lifetimes of limitations from the body and mind. I just knew I had to go to this class, and I was literally blown away with the incredible facilitation I received. It was from this point on that I made a choice to attend as many classes as possible and to completely free myself from the baggage I had carried around for far too long!

As I worked my way through the levels, I became more aware and conscious and noticed the ease, joy, lightness and expansiveness around me. I learned to ask empowering questions and to communicate with my body to include it in creating a life I would love and enjoy. Everything was changing fast, I would have clients show up for sessions, I was attending classes all over the world and travelling to new destinations, I even became a certified facilitator and taught classes and spoke at workshops and the best part for me, was promoting myself at the big exhibitions in London. I loved connecting with people and empowering them to also change their lives. It gave me a real sense of purpose. Life for me just got better and better!

Fast forward four years and I was feeling really pleased with myself for achieving so much and coming so far in my new life. It was then on that fateful morning in December 2010 when I was driving to work and I stopped at a red light that suddenly, my whole world began to fall apart and I found myself dying! Yes, you heard correctly, I thought I was dying! Sweat was dripping from every pore of my body, pins and needles spread throughout and I shook uncontrollably. The intensity was so overwhelming, I felt the angst and agitation take over and the dizziness and disorientation left me so lightheaded that it felt like I was leaving my body. My heart was pumping so hard that I thought it was going to break through my chest, leaving me in a complete state of panic!

Everything was spiralling out of control as I desperately looked around to see if there was anyone who could help me. There wasn't anyone in sight, so I knew I had to do something to pull myself together. I attempted to regulate my breathing, and to calm myself down, while at the same time, trying to do everything I could to stay focused. My only thought was to complete the last leg of my journey to work, and then, if I was going to die, at least I would be around people I knew.

I managed to make it to work and stumbled into the office. The lady I worked with saw there was something seriously wrong and immediately came to my aid. I told her what had happened and that I was worried about how I would get home later that day. The good news is that she was being very nice to me, which made a change! I spent the day relaxing and taking it easy and when it was time to go home, all these sensations and fears started to come up and I wondered if I would ever be able to make it back safely.

Driving home was a real challenge. The entire journey consisted of me bracing myself for fear of the worst happening again. When I arrived, I felt a sense of relief wash over me and I was safely home. I should mention at this point that I had made my home a safe place. I had experienced a lot of abuse in my life, so to be home meant I would not be in any danger. What I didn't know, is that this was to become a time of great change, the beginning of something new and different, a time for me to truly discover me!

After being diagnosed with a panic and anxiety disorder, I was able to leave my job, which was great, although I was to spend the next 6 years of my life living as a recluse. I was on strong medication and I would rarely go out. If I did, I would have to psyche myself up by taking myself through a mental regime of calculating the distance to get anywhere and if I would be able to get there with ease. My whole life was falling apart, I couldn't travel to give client sessions, I couldn't go out to see friends or family and I found it extremely difficult to attend classes or events. I had convinced myself that life was truly over for me, that this was going to be my reality for the rest of my life! No longer would I be able to do the things I loved and enjoyed. The only thing I knew is that no matter what was going on, I could never give up!

Choosing a greater reality

In Access, we talk about choosing a greater reality, and I knew with my current situation that I was choosing the smallest life ever! Surely this wasn't supposed to be happening to me, especially after all the classes I had attended. You're supposed to have more ease and joy, so why was this happening? Having indulged in this way of living and thinking, I began to feel restless. How could this possibly be my life forever? Was I being punished for something? These questions plagued my mind every day and at the same time, this insatiable need to remain safe was uppermost in my thoughts. It had become my number one priority! It was on this occasion that I experienced the worst attack ever. I was at home and it hit me out of nowhere. There were no warning signs and it now became clear to me that nowhere was safe, not even my home!

Nothing ever shows up that you cannot handle

I became obsessed with finding ways to overcome the panic and anxiety. I would attend every online class, workshop, one to one session, conference call and anything else that would help me in my quest. I even hired a coach who would get me to look at what I was choosing and creating as my reality. We are all infinite creators, creating our reality based on our thoughts, feelings and emotions. I started to look at and question everything, although I still couldn't figure out why this was happening to me. I was asked a great question, "What if you are exactly where you need to be right now?" "What? Really? Erm… okay. Could you say more?" It was then that my coach put it to me that nothing ever shows up that we cannot handle and then she asked me what the gift was in all of this? Wow! I had never considered this before and the lightness and expansion from hearing this, helped me to realise that this thing I had called panic and anxiety for so long was not insurmountable. I would just need to change the way I looked at it, to stop resisting it and allow myself to receive the gift it was being to me!

Your point of view creates your reality

Through my continuous dedication and commitment to using the tools of Access to change and create my life, I became aware that your point of view creates your reality. So how do you know what points of view are creating your reality? If you look at your life as it currently is, you will start to become aware of them. What points of view do you have, that are creating anxiety as your reality? Would you be willing to give them up? I've always known that our thoughts are very powerful, so when I looked at this, I saw how I was contributing to it! What a revelation!

What have you made greater than you?

What if you are far greater than you could ever imagine and what if there wasn't anything more powerful that could stop you, except you? When you make anything significant, you make it greater than you. I had given so much power to the anxiety, that it had become greater than me! It became clear in that moment that I would need to take my power back, but how? That's when I made a demand on myself that no matter what it took, I was going to change this!

I began by purchasing an online course in overcoming panic and anxiety. It had 12 modules to work through and I jumped straight in with no hesitation! After the first couple of modules, I went into huge resistance as it was suggesting I face the anxiety head on! Are they serious? Are they kidding me? Do they know what it is like to go through a panic and anxiety attack? For those of you who may not know, having a panic and anxiety attack can be likened to going through the physical motions of dying. It's not pleasant and everything becomes superimposed and intense. So, you can imagine what I was thinking when I heard this! The question is, would I be willing? I played with the idea for a while and the more I looked at it, the more I realised that if I wasn't willing to face it, I would always be at the effect of it! After getting over the initial shock, I started to question what anxiety really meant to me and what was I judging so much about it that made it difficult for me to receive beyond it?

What awareness is this giving me?

There are many tools available in Access which are designed to give you more awareness and to get you to receive with no point of view or judgement. These two things can make all the difference between having ease or difficulty with something. The choice is always ours. What would it take to live life from the space of no judgement and no point of view?

Every morning I start with lowering all my barriers and expanding my energy field out. This is a great exercise to do, as it allows you to be space, where you're not impacted by anything, including anxiety! From this space, you can begin to see clearly what's possible in going beyond any limitation you have and to change it with ease. What I became aware of is that the anxiety was not there to destroy me or my life, it was there to contribute to me becoming greater! I started to wonder what it would be like to make friends with the anxiety, instead of treating it like my worst enemy! I wonder what that would change and create?

What if everything wishes to contribute to you?

In December 2016, my son called me and asked if I would be willing to go and see my brother who was in hospital. At first, I was dubious about the whole idea. We had not spoken or seen each other for many years. We were very different, he was always angry and aggressive, whereas I was always wanting to give love and be loved. So, I looked at the energy of what it would be like if I chose to see him and it felt light. On arriving at the ward, I felt a slight tremor of anxiety emerging and trusted that everything would be okay. As soon as we saw each other, a huge wave of love came over us. He was looking very old and ill, even though he was younger than me. I immediately went up to him and held him in my arms. We were so happy, and we couldn't stop saying how much we loved each other. We had grown up in an abusive home with our mum, who kept us separate from each other and an absent alcoholic father, who we very rarely saw. As the older sister, I was protective of my brother and would save him from being picked on and bullied. So here we were, all these years later, holding each other the way I had always dreamt.

The next 6 months were to be the most precious time for me. I saw my brother often and it seemed his health was improving, and the brother and sister love we had, made life worth living for both of us. He was so much fun to hang out with. We would do all kinds of things together from going on long bike rides to buying an inflatable canoe to go on the river! It was non-stop laughter all the way! I began to realise that what was missing in my life was having fun, and the gratitude I had for my brother showing me would always be there.

It was to be a very short-lived time, as I discovered my brother had suddenly passed away, with no warning. This shook me at my very core, and it made me look at my own mortality. My anxiety levels increased, and I thought I would not be able to live my life without him. I was grateful that I could grieve for him and to be in touch with my feelings for the first time. I had spent most of my life denying my feelings, as I had to be strong, especially for my children, so to have the opportunity to do this was very liberating and helped me to heal a lot faster. I was able to receive the gift of him passing and I knew he would want me to have so much fun and to be happy. So, I made a point of choosing this in his memory.

    It was in August 2017, a month after my brother passing, that I attended a class that would prove to be a game changer. I knew I had to go, so I looked at the easiest way to get to the venue, as nothing was going to stop me, not even the anxiety! By this point, I had used all my savings, although I didn't care, as I was determined more than ever to change my life. I chose to catch a cab each day to and from the venue to make it easy on myself and during those 3 days, I was to discover things about myself I never knew! The first thing I learned is that the panic and anxiety I thought I had, was not panic and anxiety! Go figure! My head started to spin, and a lightness descended upon me.

Light and heavy

I've mentioned a few times about being light and expansive. This is just one of the many potent tools we use in Access to always know and follow what is true for us. What makes you feel light and expansive is always a truth for you and what makes you feel heavy and contractive, is always a lie for you. Have you ever felt or sensed a heaviness with panic and anxiety? Is it possible that it could be a lie for you? I invite you to consider this for a moment. During this class, I also discovered a level of potency I be that I did not want to be aware of, and which I was using against me! This explained why this intense energy that I was calling anxiety was showing up! Wow!! Wow!! Wow!! I can't tell you how happy and relieved I was to hear this! There were so many more things I learned and discovered in this class, that would change the way I would look at myself and my life.

One of the things I always struggled with was relationships, especially with men. My experiences with them weren't great, and the only good thing that came out of it was my 3 beautiful children. They were my world, and I made sure they never went without the love and affection that had been sadly missing from my life. But what about me? Do I not deserve to receive love and affection too? And would I be willing to receive this from a man? This thought felt so light. Was it possible that this could be a truth for me?

Something I haven't mentioned till now, is that I'm quite an attractive lady, although I can be very modest about this. I had spent most of my life hiding away and judging myself for not being good enough or beautiful enough, otherwise, why else would I have been abused and invalidated? This is a classic example of where your point of view creates your reality!

What I love about Access is that you choose when you're ready to choose. It's not about judging yourself if you are not willing to choose in that moment. Every choice creates an awareness, so I was happy to just be with this thought until I was ready to make a different choice.

What if choosing for you is the greatest gift?

How many of you think it is extremely selfish to choose for you? What if this is one of the lies we buy as real and true? I cannot tell you how many times I had looked at this and felt this huge resistance come up, as though it would be the crime of the century if I actually chose for me! I was living a life of lies. No wonder I was feeling all this angst in my world which left me feeling so unhappy and trapped deep down inside! What if choosing for you was the greatest gift and contribution you could ever be to you and to the world? What if now is the time to unleash you into the world? The true, authentic you?

My life has been changing so much since attending this life changing class. I no longer think about whether I will have an anxiety attack and I have been so willing to move beyond my comfort zone and to make different choices. I have been able to create a business where I get to travel with so much ease and I have noticed that the more I choose to have me in my life, the more I become an invitation to others. All this has become possible thanks to my willingness to always choose what's true and what works for me!

How much are you willing to receive?

One thing I really missed was having a companion and receiving affection, so I chose to have a beautiful pet Chihuahua, who I named Lilly. She has a very loving and playful energy about her and is such a contribution to my life. She shows me every day what it's like to have fun and she loves giving cuddles! How did I get so lucky to have her in my life?

There have been a few times where I've mentioned having a huge resistance, that could greatly contribute to my growth and expansion. Well, what if anxiety was there to contribute to you? What would that create for you, your life and your body if you didn't resist it? So, I did something I had a huge resistance to and that was registering for a cuddle workshop! The thought alone terrified and excited me all at the same time! I imagined hugging complete strangers and I knew that if I could do this, then I could do anything!

    The day of the workshop arrived, I went with a friend to make it easier and the whole journey consisted of us laughing as we imagined what it would be like. The venue was a beautiful open space and when we walked into the room, we saw a large group of people waiting for the class to begin. This could have been very overwhelming for me, triggering off an anxiety attack, but instead, I felt very calm and peaceful. The day went better than I could have imagined, we had a lot of fun with different exercises and cuddling different people. There was one guy in particular, he was so kind and I could sense he really wanted to cuddle me. He approached me and held out his hand. I took his hand and he led me to one of the mats to lie down and cuddle. This was the moment when everything changed! The workshop itself is a safe space to receive cuddles. It's non-sexual, making it a better experience to receive with no obligation. So here I was, lying with a beautiful man and cuddling him and receiving this very loving and caring energy. Something that had been missing my whole life! After 30 minutes, we thanked each other, and I floated away topped up on Oxytocin!

Since attending this workshop, I have noticed many things that have changed. The feelings and sensations associated with anxiety completely disappeared and I felt a deep connection with myself. I'm able to receive so much more and everywhere I go; people are drawn to me. I also became aware of men paying attention to me, which I had never noticed before and so I started to imagine what it would be like to be with a man who I could have fun with, and who would be kind, loving, caring, nurturing and a great contribution to my life. Just the thought alone lights me up! What if creating a life you truly desire was as simple as asking a question and just allowing yourself to wonder and imagine?

What if the purpose of life is to have fun?

I have come a long way since the beginning of this journey with anxiety and what a gift it has been. It made me very humble in recognising the truth of me and the gift and contribution I be to the world! What if you are the greatest gift that is waiting to be opened?

One of the main tools in Access is to ask questions. A question will always empower you, and an answer will always disempower you. One of my favourite questions is "What if the purpose of life is to have fun?" When I ask this question, it instantly lightens up my world! This is how I know it's true for me. So, what if the purpose of life for you is to have fun with everything you choose, including anxiety? What if fun, joy and laughter is the best medicine in healing you and the world?

I always remember an online Zoom class I attended a couple of years ago where I was asked what was true about me. At the time, I didn't have a clue, and then this lady spoke up and said she could tell just by looking at me that I was so much fun! Well, I have to admit that I have always been a fun, playful and joyful girl, although I felt it was too much for this world, as I couldn't see anyone else being that, so I decided to tone it right down! This explains a lot as to why I would have been feeling so anxious! Well, I'm happy to say I'm truly over that point of view! Every day I choose to infuse more fun and joy into my life, which has had a contagious effect on others!

So, as my story goes, this is definitely not the end! This is just the beginning of something new, amazing and wonderful! A question I would like to leave you with is "What fun, joy, laughter and excitement is there for you to discover beyond what you have decided and called anxiety?"

About Hayley Amanda Hammer

Hayley is an Empowerment Coach, Reiki Master and Intuitive Healer. She hosts a podcast show on going beyond this reality and holds special events for those who wish to experience the Access body processes for the first time at a magically reduced rate. She is also available for private sessions in person and/or online.

Her greatest wish is to see a world where people can end their suffering and struggles and begin to choose a life of ease, joy and happiness. Happy people, happy world!

Hayley is also offering a free guided exercise for dealing with anxiety and a free 30-minute consultation. For more information or to book a session, you can visit her site at: www.accessnewbeginnings.com

Thanxiety
by Carolyn Street

Thanxiety: from worried and stuck to resilient and resourceful. How to settle the symptoms, find the right help and transform it from an adversary to an ally. Seven simple and effective ways to help yourself out of a bout of anxiety. Learn how to ease worry on the spot easily, without having to move or find equipment.

Here are some practical, no-maintenance just-in-time actions and remedies that work to alleviate anxiety in the here and now. To be used when anxiety is a reality in the moment. You can do these anytime, anywhere while help (if needed) is on its way.

I love rhymes so I put them together to the tune of 'if you're happy and you know it'. Sing along or read them aloud or to yourself.

If you're anxious and you know it deep-breathe in,
count to four, hold for four and then breathe out
if you're anxious and you know it
but you really want to throw it
in the bin just breathe air in and breathe air out.

If you're anxious and you know it hold a thumb
Left or right it doesn't matter hold a thumb
if you're anxious and you know it

but you really want to throw it
in the bin the easy win is hold a thumb.

If you're anxious and you know it hug yourself
cross your arms and hold your armpits hug yourself
and you know you've really got this
have to give yourself some love
'the big hug' is just the ticket hug yourself.

If you're anxious and you know it tap your nose
7 times give or take you tap your nose
even though it feels quite silly
have a go, it helps with the willies
if you're anxious and you know it tap your nose.

If you're anxious and you feel it look straight up
you can raise your eyebrows, smile and look straight up
if you're anxious and you feel it
look straight up it helps to sort it
if you're anxious – you can do it - look straight up.

If you're anxious and you know it walk to hope
Start where you are, step to neutral then to hope
this is called 'Chaining Anchors'
Go on and try it, it's the dope
If you're anxious and you know it walk to hope

If you're anxious and you know it say thank you
Cos there's nothing like a spot of gratitude
If you're anxious it's because your mind
is only trying to help
Say 'thank you, mind, what's next? and all is well.

I have simplified the tools to be accessible in times of anxiety whether low-grade up to even panic attack while waiting for help or for the immediate term as a sort of First Aid. Depending on your mental bandwidth at the time, they can be more effective and efficient in the moment in the expanded forms. We can move on now to elaborate on each of the to-dos. My priority is to keep things simple and as generic as possible; further information and reading is available on my website and in the resources list.

I recommend that you read through the instructions and brief explanations that follow and shortlist 1 or 2 that you like the most.

Remedy One - Breathing

Have you noticed your breathing change when you feel anxious? We tend to hold our breath, breathe really shallowly or begin to hyperventilate the more anxious we get. Remembering to breathe and making the breath even calms the heart and nervous system. Once you have remembered to breathe start to even out the phases of breathing. This technique is known as square breathing. Breathe in to the count of four, hold it for four, breathe out for four and hold for four. There are numerous other breathing techniques but I find this one the easiest to remember and the most calming.

Remedy 2 - Holding A Thumb

We are born with instincts to cope with life. It is probably safe to say that the vast majority of babies suck their thumbs. The energy meridians in the thumbs correspond to stress and anxiety. Sucking a thumb is like putting jumper cables to the ports of a battery that help the energy circuit to have a boost and get going again once it has been depleted. External stressors and our thought processes can deplete those energies. Grown-ups can simply wrap one hand around the thumb of the other hand to settle the nerves and calm anxious responses down. It doesn't matter which one you hold; you might hold one first then the other. There are theories that say we should hold the left first then the right as the left is associated with the past and the right is more to do with the present and future but simplicity is the priority. And if you want extra comfort, remember you are an adult and no one has the authority to tell you to stop sucking your thumb; should you feel so inclined.

Remedy 3 - The Big Hug

This self-hug is a variation of the usual one. If you slide your right hand into your left armpit and your left hand into your right armpit you connect the energy pathways. If you bring your thumbs out so they are in a sort of thumbs-up gesture, and press lightly inwards into the 3rd rib from the top on either side, that boosts an energy circuit that helps clear confusion and brings clarity. If any of these techniques seem awkward or tricky move on to the next one as we need to avoid adding worry over not doing things 'correctly'.

Remedy 4 - Tapping On Your Nose

Tapping while saying a phrase describing an emotional state has been around for decades and has many forms. 7 is the number of perfection and it is the number of times I tend to tap when I use this technique. I find counting adds stress, some people find counting comforting. See what works for you.

For quick relief from anxiety tap the tip of the nose while saying 'I'm anxious' and then a 'because' phrase followed by 'and it's all right'. That is the easy version and easy is best when we need to decrease mental activity. The tip of the nose is on the energy line that goes with our destiny and purpose. It also converges with the line that harmonises mental and emotional energies. So tapping on it gently activates our awareness of our purpose which helps us see the source of the anxiety in perspective and helps us access a more resourceful state. The nose is one of a whole set of beneficial tapping points and the set that I recommend is available in the resources list.

Remedy 5 - Looking Upwards

Our eyes move in different directions to access information from the brain. It is very difficult to feel negative if you look upwards. You can experiment by looking downwards; chances are you will begin to feel the more heavy and unpleasant emotions. Now try moving your eyes sideways and diagonally. These movements are included in the 'Brain Gym' method and in some forms of the tapping technique. Moving the eyes around connects the dots of awareness and again, directly accesses our resourcefulness so we can regain a sense of proportion and find a balanced approach to the issue at hand. There is a saying that goes 'emotions up, intelligence down'.

Remedy 6 - Chaining Anchors or as I call it 'Walk to Hope'

In other words from 'Anxious and Alarmed To Calm, Self-Belief and Trust, Optimism and Hope; Gratitude, even'. This is another one that can be done on the spot. It requires some space. Stand up and imagine you are on a stepping stone. We will call this one the stone of doom.

Ahead of you are four more stepping stones. Look ahead to the last stepping stone and make a mental note that is the stepping stone of hope, optimism, calm confidence, resourcefulness and ease with the situation. On the stone of doom make a list of all the factors that are causing you anxiety. When you have taken stock you will realise that it feels less negative. When you are ready, step to the next stepping stone. We will call this one the stone of gloom. Gloom feels better than doom, doesn't it? So it is still a negative and worried space with 'what-if this' and 'what-if that' and some overthinking. Once you have acknowledged that those thoughts are there you will feel ready to move to the stone of in-between. This is the stone of realism and rationality; neither negative nor positive. You can spend as long as you like on each stone. Move ahead only when you are ready.

Then, you guessed it; you step to slightly positive – this can be called the 'yes, but' stone. Finally on to the last one which is the goal. At the stone of hope, optimism and gratitude you can see how your anxiety was a helpful ally; it alerted you that something was wrong and indicated that you needed to change your thinking purposefully and carefully. Taking your mind off something doesn't make it go away; with this approach we get to see the issues for what they are, challenges and gain the mental resilience and courage to be open to the solution.

Remedy 7 – Gratitude

We have heard of the benefits of gratitude lists. Putting the mind in a state of gratitude is truly effective as your mind works to keep you safe and well. If it is producing anxiety and you say thank you for helping, please turn the volume down, it will recognise that you have received the alert message (the anxiousness). Then it will reduce the intensity of the signal (the physiological signs of anxiety will decrease) and calm will set in enabling the third phase, action to follow on.

This is a practical way of working with the Emotional Scale which is wonderfully covered in another chapter, with a slight twist in that you are using your body and what we call Total Physical Response to actively move yourself to your goal-state. Standing and walking activate the energies associated with motivation and a can-do approach with confidence. When we are anxious we normally sit or lie down. Sitting down for prolonged periods disharmonises the energies that work with our faith and optimism thus increasing anxiety and its action, worry. The saying 'sitting is the new smoking' alludes to this. An example of this is cabin fever in flights.

So standing and walking the sequence from doom to gloom to neutral to all right to positive optimism, resourcefulness and hope is a very effective way of getting ourselves out of anxiety and into a conducive, can-do motivated frame of mind body and heart. The desired state; hopeful, confident, optimistic, positive is the true north. First to get out of the negative and into neutral. Then to positive and to the even higher energies.

Testing Out The Tools - My Testimony

The last time I had an anxiety attack was June 2017. I was waiting to disembark a plan at the stopover. We'd been delayed and I was worried about catching the next flight as the boarding gate seemed to be very far off. We had just realised that we hadn't booked accommodation in London, our final destination, for the night. My elderly mum was feeling unwell and the trigger was the airline's theme song which for some reason provoked dizziness, mental fog, nausea and a complete loss of control. I used a combination of these in that very tight, chaotic spot (people opening and closing the overhead bins, some pushing past, the nausea becoming overwhelming). I could not sit down as an elderly lady had taken my seat. I was stuck in this flurry. It passed within 2 minutes (I know because my mum and I did them together and we timed ourselves). Once compos mentis thanks to the tools, I was able to work out how to get help and in the end we made our way to the next boarding gate with time to spare.

How Anxiety Shows Up For Me And My Anxiety Story In A Nutshell.

In my case anxiety happens as follows. Soundbytes in the form of disjointed phrases people have said to me in the past or things I heard said around me take over my mind and play loudly in my head like a broken record. Sometimes my own utterances start to replay ominously, which gets me alarmed as I start to worry about something I may have been unclear about. I worry about the consequences.

It's usually one at a time but sometimes they link to other similar quotes or soundbytes which can seem perfectly neutral. There is never any 'commentary' nor are there any external nor judgmental voices, which some people experience. In my case they are always things I clearly remember having heard. The volume can be alarming and I will start to realise this is going on and start paying attention. That is when the problem or issue my mind is trying to alert me to will come clear, I realise what the underlying problem is that the soundbytes relate to and that is when the worry starts. Sometimes it fits the description of 'analysis paralysis.

These soundbytes can be disjointed phrases I have heard people say which my mind starts to reinterpret in a string of different ways. At other times I realise I have been fixating on an issue for some time without any change and that mental discomfort can be quite extreme. Anxiety also strikes in instances of overwhelm. When I am trying to put tasks in a sequence, I get anxious, things get overcomplicated and panic can ensue. This started earlier than I can remember.

My exploration of anxiety began when I was a child, worrying about my parents when they were out at business or social occasions at night time or out late for work. At times I would worry if they began arguing. I started my own serious research in my teens when I realised nobody understood me not least because by the time I got the chance to speak to someone, the thoughts had vanished or diminished in seriousness and I couldn't articulate what had been wrong. I realised I had to help myself. Anxiety is a hidden condition and I seemed perfectly well-adjusted at boarding school, university and teacher training in Modern Foreign Languages and Sociology. I had no phobias nor was I ever unhealthy.

I returned to Singapore in the late 1990s and began working as a German – English translator. I joined the teaching staff at a local polytechnic. It was my dream job for 17 years. I had become devoted to my other passion, public speaking by that point and was head of the public speaking module. I had raving reviews from my students for my ability to help them overcome their nerves and gain confidence. I had no qualms travelling overseas with large groups of students and I had the nickname 'the singing French teacher'. I spent my free time at seminars and workshops on self-help, alternative and complimentary healing therapies to find ways both to understand my at times still debilitating anxiety so as to help myself and others.

With the tools I learned and mastered, I was able to manage the anxiety which kept bubbling under the surface most of the time. Sometimes, however I would be triggered by the increasing demands of administrative work which involved sequencing tasks and spreadsheets. I decided to become a therapist which I finally did in 2017 when my contract ended.

In Summary

Anxiety is a natural phenomenon and given the right sort of attention with a carefully caring attitude and space, with the right sort of processing, it can be seen for what it truly is; a gift in disguise. The mental discomfort, dizziness, palpitations, looping thoughts and a feeling of being stuck in one's head are just a few of the features of that disguise. What if anxiety just needs those symptoms to get our attention?

A Word About Chemical Anti-Anxiety Drugs

I knew I would never use anti-anxiety medication; I had seen too many people experience adverse effects. I will not discuss drugs here as there are ethical restrictions. I dedicate this chapter to those who lost their zest for life, their joie de vivre and sometimes their own agency because of drugs that numbed and dumbed them down. Again, take your medical practitioner's advice.

I titled this chapter 'Thanxiety' because without it we would not know that there is something wrong with our thinking. It is important to ask the right questions and be able to process the answers and pace and lead ourselves up to a point of understanding how to course-correct our thought processes. We must be able to neutralise the discomfort that is symptomatic of serious anxiety in order to reframe it and regain our resourcefulness. If we simply reframe the worry or anxiety we fail to see the issue as it is and may overlook something that requires caution or further rational thought. As has been shared in other chapters, Access Consciousness® has some wonderful clearing statements and questions that help to steer the mind away from the negative feelings surrounding anxiety and towards more useful ways of thinking. 'What's good or right about this that I'm not getting?' is my favourite clearing statement when I feel anxiety coming on. NLP uses reframes and a tool I love especially called 'Perceptual Positions' which helps alleviate anxiety caused by not knowing how ones actions have been interpreted by others.

If I had not been curious about my anxiety and started seeing it as a project not a problem, as Mary Burmeister of Jin Shin Jyutsu®) recommends, I would not have been able to solve my own high anxiety let alone help others including my clients.

Treating Anxiety In Others
by Carolyn Street

Introduction

I have been a full-time therapist and coach since 2017. When working with anxiety it is important to understand that because we are working with thoughts, which are transitory, it is challenging to articulate the problem to someone who is unfamiliar with the condition. I found that my own anxiety caused me to speak very fast and pack my speech with more information than my audience – even some therapists - could digest. (Side note: when someone says I talk to fast I quip 'you listen too slow', a topic for another book). The key is to be 'carious'; curious about the person's issue and caring enough to hear them out and make extra effort to understand that they are trying to express something that is in its essence, difficult to articulate.

My specialism is anxiety, specifically self-expression anxiety public speaking and confidence-coaching. I work with relationship anxiety and social anxiety amongst other labels. Sessions start with a discussion of the issue or issues that the client has come seeking help with. Based on that discussion I suggest a course of interactive treatment which includes one or more of the following (further information available at the links provided at the end of this chapter).

- Hypnotherapy - the Marisa Peer Method® otherwise known as Rapid Transformational Therapy®
- Jin Shin Jyutsu® - as presented by Mary Burmeister and her lineage
- NeuroLinguistic Programming® - selectively
- My adaptation of the tapping approach; Emotional Freedom Technique with Attitude
- Access Consciousness® clearing statements and body processes

Section 1: What is anxiety?

In short, it's the absence of self-love. In general, anxiety takes over when a person forgets to love themself and focusses on external things or things beyond their control. It is an umbrella term for overthinking about the same thing or things to a point where it becomes an issue in itself; shame, embarrassment, inability to sequence tasks, preoccupation with something so that other things that require thought go forgotten. It can show up as appetite imbalances, inner unease and/or worry over unknown consequences of past events and prolonged thinking 'what-if' as well as an overactive mind. It can have a known cause or not. Usually it is connected with experiences from the past and the thought process relating to the present. Sometimes it is something related to the future but is usually very much in the present moment; when we ruminate and cannot decide whether to take action or not and if so, what action to take. We have to think to find solutions in our day to day lives so quitting thinking is not an option. We are hard-wired to be problem-solvers and worrying is trying to solve problems with the wrong approach.

Some people do not think enough and that is also an imbalance. The 'Just Do It' approach can have extremely damaging consequences. In my blended therapy practice I see clients everyday who have experienced adverse consequences after doing things without the requisite forethought and preparation. As the saying goes 'I think therefore I am'. Anxiety is when that thinking becomes a disturbance or when the thoughts cannot naturally flow but get stuck. When one can get to a place of self-love, one can prioritise one's mental well-being and only then can the causes of anxiety be seen in perspective and addressed with resourcefulness so that the focus is no longer on the problems but to solutions.

Side note: Anxiety is different from fear, though some symptoms can overlap; fear is the awareness of danger posed by an identifiable threat.

A Client Story

A new client, Dominic (not his real name) called for a strategy session prior to signing up for a package with me. He was extremely well-spoken and extremely gentlemanly on the phone. He wanted help with public speaking and performance anxiety. He had started a new job, one which he had wanted very much and was delighted with. There were two problems which he rated 8.5 on a scale of 10, 10 being extremely severe; panic attack level. Both issues were brand new to him. The first was that he had started to get extremely nervous to the point of sweating and stuttering when making sales presentations. He had realised that the trigger was when his boss or a colleague who was familiar with the topic and specialist information was present. The anxiety alarmed him in itself as well as because he had always been very confident with presentations in the past. He mentioned that he had always been able to 'wing it' no matter who the audience comprised of nor the subject matter.

The second problem was that he had developed an intense distaste for his own voice. He had seen two hypnotherapists before me and was almost desperate for help. I put him in a light hypnotic trance. He 'went back' to a scene at school aged twelve in which he had dozed off and woken up minutes before he was due to play his clarinet at a school recital. He had meant to practice but had fallen asleep instead. Having rushed to the venue he was scolded by the music teacher for being late and in the wrong uniform. On that occasion his performance had been just above average and he was given another chance to redeem himself at the next recital. He practiced for that occasion and played excellently. The learning from that scene was that he needed to be better prepared for his sales presentations and could no longer 'wing it'. Like many extroverts he did not like to prepare and plan for his presentations. He realised that this had to change.

I worked with him to develop a work plan that suited him such that he would schedule preparation time prior to each presentation. We also practiced my method of rehearsing. He realised that he had been rushing through these presentations as he was anxious not to take up too much time and bore the other representatives from the regional offices or the companies he was pitching to. This in turn was due to the fact that he would get terribly bored while they spoke at length and took up what was to him far too much time. Having realised this he began to get used to speaking more slowly and steadily. He noticed that his peers began to give him positive feedback when he gave more details and elaboration in his presentations. The best thing of all was that when he spoke slowly and steadily he was able to adopt an authoritative tone. He began to appreciate the sound of his voice again and all was well.

The Importance Of Working On Alleviating Anxiety

Beyond enabling us to gain clarity, freedom from the symptoms and to return to self-love and stability, there are greater reasons to keep anxiety in check. As ancient wisdom has had it for thousands of years and science is discovering to be true, emotions and our inner state are the cause of medical issues and even diseases. In the school of thought I align with, Jin Shin Jyutsu® which I discuss at length on my various social media and other platforms, anxiety and the act of worrying without adequate balancing and processing is the cause of diseases like diabetes and appetite-related illnesses. Those of us with a tendency to overthink, worry, be lost in our mental chatter and so on have to be very careful not to let information like that make us more alarmed and anxious as that defeats the whole point.

The Role and Function Of Skilled Reframing

This is why the Emotional Scale by Esther and Jerry Hicks / Abraham is so brilliant. In psychology trying to change ones perspective of something from a negative view to a positive view is called a reframe. It means looking at something as a positive rather than as something negative. For example the advice we often hear from non-worriers to 'let go, let God' is called a reframe leap; it is too far of a jump. It is possible (and useful) to go from worried to sad to angry and so on step by step but if you try to jump from anxious to happy and securely contented and confident then that could cause a fall to a more negative state rather than a step up in the right direction.

Section 2: How To Be A Friend To Someone With Anxiety And When And How To Select A Therapist

Friends are great and most of us have at least one best friend; a confidant with a ready listening ear at most hours of need. Most people attribute the fear of speaking to a fear of being misunderstood or judged (which is overly simplistic and for another book). If someone is talking about their anxiety, do not judge them. When I am not working and friends come to me with issues I am acutely aware that they need me to function as that shoulder to cry on or sounding board and often, just to be there. Sometimes they need me to cheer them up or help them see a way to be more fair and kind to themselves. That is my favourite thing to do, bring joy to people. I know what it is like to suffer and, like Robin Williams, would rather be the cheery clown than let someone stay down.

Sometimes it is to empathise and validate them, restore their self-esteem and help them process their issues in a sharing is caring sort of a way. The bond and trust that friends share is invaluable. What is the difference between a friend and a coach or therapist though?

A professional is duty-bound to have the needs, safety and growth as their priority. A friend without the skills and astuteness of a professional may unintentionally fail to pick up on a serious issue in the moment. Also friends are not necessarily equipped to cope with something another friend shares as it may trigger emotions and adverse reactions in themselves. In a shared space or context if friend A wants to talk about something specific, friend B and others if others are present, need to be able to hold the space for A to talk, share, vent or simply express him or herself in that environment of shared trust and warmth. If however the other friend or friends are not sensitive to A's needs they may change the subject too soon. Some even do what I call 'emotional one-upmanship' by interrupting and sharing a story of their own which they believe has more emotional value or upset-value than A's. A, having needed the attention and care at the time might leave feeling worse than before. This comes under the term 'confider's regret' which I will pick up on later. Friends are also not professionally and ethically bound to confidentiality and most of us know what the consequences of that can look like.

Equally, it is important not to engage in 'trauma-bonding'. Hobb's Law states that neurons that fire together wire together. If your friend is overly relating to your issue then that 'validation' without proper healing or processing towards a learning outcome can serve to just make the effects of the issue deeper entrenched.

Section 3: When And How To Find Your Ideal Therapist

So if you feel like your friends have already done their best or your friends are not the sort of people you would confide in and trust to find you the best solutions for you, start your search for a therapist that suits you.

First, know your needs. Do you want someone who will be able to really understand you yet keep enough distance so as to see how you can course-correct and suggest the right techniques, modalities and approaches for you to best reach your desired goals and outcomes?

You must know yourself. Are you more extroverted or introverted? My favourite frameworks for this are adaptations of Trompenaars Hampden-Turner's 7 Dimensions of Culture and Ron Kaufmann's 5 communication styles from his 'UP! Your Service' books and courses, both of which I used to facilitate as an in-house trainer at arguably the most beautiful educational institution in Singapore.

Do you have to talk about a subject and piece together the factors and details before you get to the point? Or are you the other way round; able to pinpoint the main issue in a nutshell then find that the context is useful?

Are you expressive? Do you prefer someone who will respond empathetically and interject during gaps in your train of thought to demonstrate that they are there for you, listening and available with their full attention? Someone who might share their own insights or short anecdotes to show that they can relate and know where you are coming from? It is important that the focus remains on you throughout. Or would you prefer someone who remained unmoved and neutral who may ask the odd clarifying question but otherwise lets you talk?

Do you feel comfortable and safe with people who are similar to you or with people who you can see differences with? This can be a subconscious form of discernment but is important.

Do you value experience or accreditation or both? Some therapists refer to themselves as experienced experts. I believe that some accreditation is important.

Are you more past, present or future-orientated in your thoughts and communication? If you are past-oriented and the therapist is solely future-oriented there may be dissonance as the therapist will likely be unable to relate to your need to be brought out of that tendency towards a more future-positive perspective. For example I have experienced a few therapists who will cut me short mid-explanation of my issue. My intention is to provide all the facts and necessary details so they can be fully informed. It is too much of a leap for me to perceive how advice like 'stop worrying; worry is a prayer for what you don't want' if I do not know how to stop the worry for one and know what I do want, so as to focus on that, for another. Conceptually it makes sense but to me I begin to worry that the worry I have been doing has been manifesting what I don't want all along.

Does the therapist walk the talk?

One of the main prerequisites for me is that the therapist has benefitted from and believes in the modalities they practice. There are many coaching, therapy and counselling outfits out there. I know of one or two practitioners of energy work who do not ever receive the therapies they themselves practice for profit. In our therapy school students begin to work on each other as client and therapist from day one, working on real issues. This can be done because of the quality of the programme. We are also given the resources to practice on each other with our real issues. As a lively collaborating community we have resources like Facebook groups where we can seek second opinions and others' inputs when we have clients with issues we have not dealt with before. Doctors and medical staff have to keep up to date with best practices and also receive treatment. The same should go for mental health workers and therapists.

Many people value certifications, academic qualifications and scientific accolades. Do framed certificates from esteemed universities inspire confidence? Or are you more inclined to want a therapist who has experienced similar issues, is able to empathise yet be professional and client-centred? There are licensed therapists who have never treated a real client until they are actually working with one as their first case in their first therapy practice.

When searching for a therapist ensure that you are clear about what therapy entails. I had a client who wanted to have her father and husband in the room during her initial session. They were insistent that it would be fine and only for the first session. She wanted to cure her irregular heartbeat anxiety and low thyroid function levels. I had successfully worked with several clients with similar issues by that point. I relented and made an exception. During the session she would stop to ask her husband or father to verify information pertaining to her symptoms. I had to interject several times, albeit gently. In hypnosis she realised that her issues were due to excessive familial pressure as a new daughter-in-law and mother. She stopped her processing due to their being present. In subsequent sessions she could not settle down as she was missing her husband and children. As a family they would be together always when at home. It was a cultural custom. She was what is referred to as communitarian. Therapy works best when one is aware of and secure in one's own agency, for more modern cultures where individualism is the norm. The results for her were satisfactory; her arrhythmia and anxiety improved but the effects were not as great as they normally are. In hindsight I should have referred her to counselling for co-dependency.

Confider's Confidence Versus Confider's Regret

An ideal therapist fosters confider's confidence, not confider's regret. The result should be confider's contentment as the client should leave the session feeling empowered and confident, relieved of their burden of anxiety with the tools to act in self-love. I have coined these terms because they speak to my main prerequisite for effective mental health professionals. A client should feel empowered, motivated and hopefully inspired after a therapy session. If a therapist doesn't enable the client to feel safe, comfortable and understood then confider's regret can set in, especially if the client is a sensitive person. It takes courage to be vulnerable. I have felt varying degrees of embarrassment or shame and oftentimes 'being made wrong' after sharing personal information that was received with what I perceived as disapproval or boredom or judgment by the therapist. To me I was providing information that was key to understanding my issue. Some therapists can even be dismissive of information offered by clients and that can cause confider's regret as the client can feel like a burden; that they have talked too much and inconvenienced or bored the therapist. I call that out as shameful and highly unprofessional.

The Pros and Pitfalls Of 'Pattern Interrupting'

Many highly effective coaches and therapy professionals believe in 'pattern interrupting'. In other words this means stopping a client's train of thought and changing the subject if it seems to the professional that they have gone off-tangent or are being unnecessarily long-winded or taking too much time. Without carefully assessing the vulnerability and emotional resilience of the client, this can backfire. At the very least this is very short-sighted and in terms of effectiveness and use of time, the equivalent of 'penny-wise and pound foolish'. It is far more worthwhile being thorough with a client's history, paying attention to his or her language, non-verbals and thought-processing in order to be able to treat the client as the unique individual that he or she is. A client frequently will always be able to process better if given the space and conducive, safe environment to express him or herself. In many ways they are right to do so with tact, sensitivity, courtesy and with full respect to the client's needs.

If a client is repeating themselves or not taking my cues to allow the session to make progress then I will alert them as that repetition can be counterproductive. Hobb's Law states that the more we repeat something the more it becomes a belief then a conviction. The imprint gets deeper. Repeating a story over and over again just deepens the emotions associated with it. This is another reason why using the tools and seeking and following through with the right help for you is so important.

The Right Balance Of Relatability

Confider's regret can also occur when the professional is overly relatable or thinks they know all about the client's issue or issues. They over-identify in an attempt to make the client feel understood. This can have the opposite effect. If the professional has had the same experience they can develop immunity to the perceived seriousness and mismatch the client by being or seeming dismissive. No two people experience the same events the same way. They may use convoluted terms or jargon and undermine the client's right to understand the issue. The client has no means of proceeding with the right information and clarity. I had a health coach who was very good at guiding me where to find resources for my thyroid condition and related issues that would suit my interest levels and discuss them with me as someone of equal intelligence but different expertise.

Many clients have experienced a few therapists previously and the reason they did not find those therapists' work effective was because they did not feel like they were given the space and attention to explain the issue thoroughly enough to their satisfaction. As was the case with Dominic.

One question that crops up is 'so you are just a friend with solutions?' Yes and no and in between. Some clients do not want a friend. The key requisite is professional distance. It is a balance between being someone the client is comfortable to talk to about anything who is able to professionally deal with it (and not take it on or be emotionally affected by it) and having the skills to listen on the one hand and work out solutions and next steps on the other.

When extreme emotions and hurt involved however, a friend can say or do something that causes further hurt or at the very worst, cause confider's regret and even shame in the person with the issue. There is also the issue of confidentiality; a therapist is ethically bound to treat information shared by their clients as sacrosanct (unless the client mentions hurting a vulnerable person or ideations of suicide).

The Pros And Cons Of Context

Other clients do not mention key issues believing that they might be judged or stereotyped by the therapist. Then there is the risk of proceeding without crucial information which ultimately wastes time. If a client is not sharing all the pertinent details this can hinder or even mislead the course of therapy and the outcome may even be an adverse one. The onus is on the therapist to ensure that all relevant factors and information is given by the client and properly understood by the therapist.

In short the 3 criteria for a good therapist-client relationship are 'know, like, trust'. As a client it is your responsibility to make sure that your chosen therapist is all 3 of those. Do due diligence to ensure that you really value the skills, abilities, experiences and personality of your chosen therapist. My advice is to check out 3 therapists with credentials and testimonials that you align with.

Gaining An Attitude Of Gratitude

As the poet, writer and equal-opportunities activist Audre Lorde said 'When I dare to be powerful, when I use my strength in the service of my vision, then it becomes less and less important whether I am afraid'. I interpret 'afraid' in this quote as encompassing anxiety and turning it into productive self-love. Working with anxiety as an ally by alleviating the negative aspects of it and exploring what it had to teach me - and by extension my clients in their unique journeys - became my purpose. I discovered public speaking and its healing, restorative powers when exercised in tandem with the careful space-holding and growth and empowering environment I outlined above. In my practice I help people overcome all sorts, shapes and forms of anxiety and other conditions.

We can be thankful for the gift of anxiety once we have come to view it as a useful signal that we need to explore our thinking and find ways that suit us as individuals towards solutions. Who knows who we can help and we can start with ourselves.

Thanks, Anxiety. Thank you God and thank you reader for being part of the solution; one by one we can harmonize anxiety into self-love for the good of all.

If you are not safe or there are others in your care or you are at all at risk then make sure you call for help and get to a safe space. Do not risk passing out or endangering yourself. If you are driving or operating machinery stop immediately and get help.

About Carolyn Street

Carolyn's bucket list has 3 legacy goal-type items on it , one of which is the "And Us" series, this being the very first instalment. She also wants to start and grow a mobile therapy business where clients get coaching, acupressure or hypnotherapy on the road, by rail, or in the air, on the way from A to B.

When she isn't helping clients with their projects around anxiety, sadness, anger, fear and frustration, Carolyn runs public speaking programmes tailored to her clients' individual sets of needs incorporating therapy where appropriate.

COVID 19 brought Carolyn a set of stresses, challenges and even tragic loss. On the bright side, she has become quite a homebody, an absolute miracle by some standards!

Her 'hobbies' are an extension of her work with the odd hot yoga lesson, dancing on her rebounder, energy work for the planet and acrylic painting.

Carolyn is active on Facebook, her basic website is at www.holisticcoachsg.com and she is looking forward to interacting with readers in the "And Us" Facebook group.

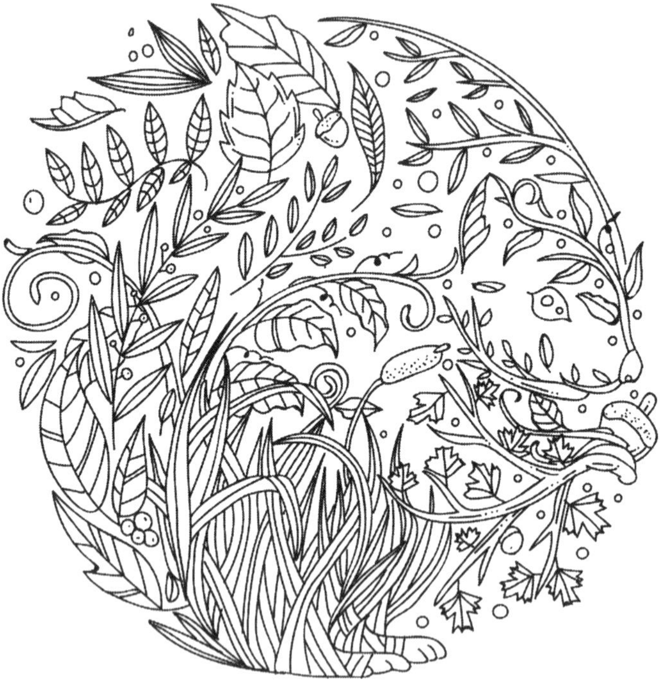

A Hero's Journey
by Martin Seville

Definitions

"You're depressed and have high anxiety." That's what the doctor said. Shaking, heart pounding, feeling sick, with a stadium of voices screaming in my mind and what felt like a vice compressing my head, I sat there like a lost child in the small but functional doctor's room.

Depressed sounded right, after all I did feel very low. Anxiety though? Anxious? I wasn't so sure. Stressed, worried, overwhelmed, exhausted - definitely. Anxious, however, just didn't seem like the right word. Maybe a definition would help …

anxiety noun (WORRY)
an uncomfortable feeling of nervousness or worry about something that is happening or
might happen in the future.
Cambridge Dictionary

Ah! Ok. That does sounds right. I worried about everything and apparently, that's anxiety. Definitions aside, why was this such a surprise? It's interesting looking back on it. Today we live and work in what seems like a world of anxiety. It appears everywhere, is more openly talked about and it's one of the conditions I now help people with.

At that time though, "anxiety" just wasn't the word that was used. Everything was "stress"; maybe for many, it still is.

Do words really matter though? I tend to think so, because the clearer we can describe what we are feeling, the easier it is for someone to help. "Stressed", for example, is so commonly used today that it's normalised, misunderstood and even devalued. There's a huge difference between being a little stressed and being so stressed that you just don't know what to do. In my experience, the more stressed and anxious you are, the less likely you are to talk about it. You could say, it's the quiet ones you need to look out for.

Anyway, where were we? Ah yes, looking up the definition of anxiety after my initial doubts, only to be described perfectly by the Cambridge Dictionary and, therefore, promptly corrected.

Please make it stop

This was the start of a long period of treatment, diagnosis and recovery. This was the point at which things had got so bad I could barely function. The point at which, against everything I had previously believed about overcoming stress without medication, I was desperate to be given something, anything that could help. To make the screaming and pounding stop. To make the feeling that my body was going to explode, stop. Please.

It's fair to say I'd left it rather late. The warning signs had been there for years; but, of course, I could soldier on, I would survive, others had it much worse. My British stiff upper lip was in full effect and let's face it - I should be grateful for a good job and loving family. Oh, the stories we tell ourselves that keep us in unhealthy situations.

That kind of attitude was all well and good (well, not really) … until it was too late, and my body took the ability to do anything about my anxiety out of my hands. It started shutting down. That was unpleasant; to put it mildly.

I was sat at my desk looking at my computer, in a large glass corporate building, surrounded by people in suits, conference calls, and the noise of keyboards tapping and photo-copy-printers whirring. That's when and where it happened … Full Burnout.

There was nothing I could do about it. Nothing. I was rooted to the spot, couldn't move, couldn't talk. Head painfully screaming, uncontrollably shaking, blurry vision, heart pounding, sick to my stomach, temperature rising … and I had absolutely no idea what was going on. It was terrifying to lose control in such a way; and terrifying to think this could happen anywhere. In some ways I was lucky – I could have been driving. A large open office, full of people, however, still wasn't exactly ideal. My body, however, wasn't messing around; this was a serious warning shot. It was saying loudly and clearly:

"We cannot cope anymore with what you've been putting us through. The strategies you've been using to cope no longer work. We're shutting you down. You need immediate help."

It was a very effective message. If I had been savvy enough to read between the lines, I'd have also realised that I had already done serious harm to my one and only body and the road to recovery from this point was going to be long and certainly not easy. Unfortunately, I wasn't savvy. It's true I was desperate to be given something that could help me get back to some resemblance of myself; the mental and physical strain was exhausting. The incentive, however, was less about my long-term health. It was more about quickly returning to the mindset that had got me in this position in the first place. In the cold light of day that clearly makes no sense, so allow me to explain, for it's a trap so many of us fall into.

Unquestionable truth

Being ill or injured, in any measure, is … inconvenient. There we are merrily getting on with our lives and wham we're suddenly required to start looking after ourselves to return to full health. (Hint: Read that again.) Then, sometimes, our bodies and even minds have the sheer audacity to hit us so hard that we need to STOP! That's beyond inconvenient; that's extremely selfish! They should know better than anyone about our 100 priorities, our projects, our deadlines, our pressures, our bills to pay, our family to look after, our performance review, the forthcoming work restructures … the list goes on … and that's without Great Aunt Doris' birthday preparations!

When life is moving so fast, we don't have time to STOP! When we've got projects and deadlines to hit, we don't have time to STOP! When we're working every hour, even at the known detriment to our health and relationships, we still have no time to STOP! We need to work. We need to keep our job. We need to pay the mortgage. We need to think and act like we are because there is no other way. It will take only one piece of the puzzle to go missing to unravel our entire lives. That's the unquestionable truth we believe.

This is what keeps us trapped in a whole host of things in life - like unhealthy habits, routines, mindsets, relationships and jobs. All this creates … anxiety … and what underpins much of this is something arguably even more sinister … fear. The fear of losing what we have. The fear of not being good enough. The fear of failure. This fear pushes us to our very limits; and sometimes beyond.

Learn and adapt
So, with all of this in mind, what happened next? Well actually, the conversation that started this very chapter. Then there were a few days off – naturally there was no way I was going to allow myself to be "signed off" and have that on my work record. (Hint: Acting out of fear.) On a more positive note, anti-depressants were prescribed to help clear my head, and incredible courses attended to understand 'Low Mood', 'Stress', 'Anxiety, Sleep and Mindfulness' – all run by the amazing Gloucestershire 2gether NHS Foundation Trust. Just some of the important lessons I learnt included:
- Journaling to identify triggers that impacted me negatively – this enabled me to choose whether to avoid the trigger or practice a healthier, more positive response.

- The link between my thoughts, emotions and behaviours – and that I always had a choice on how to react to any situation.
- Incorporate 3 things into my day: 1) Achieve something, 2) Do something positive for me, and 3) Have some meaningful human interaction.
- Think and act on facts – mind reading, judgements, predicting, catastrophising, shoulds and musts all lead to fear and anxiety – facts are my friend.
- It also became clear that anxiety was a very natural process and that a bad moment doesn't mean a bad day, week, month or life.

These lessons I still practice today. I was also afforded flexibility by my workplace – working from home to reduce the exhaustion of my 2 hour daily commute, flexibility in the mornings and even working the hours of 10 days in 9 so I could have an extra day off every other week.

All these things eased pressure, exhaustion, improved knowledge and taught me strategies. I highly recommend all of them. Do listen to your doctor. Do learn about your condition. Do work with your workplace. I guess, therefore, here ends our tale. All sorted. Job done. Life moves on. We all "lived happily ever after". Roll credits. Unfortunately, not quite.

Not again

All of this bought me 20 months … before burnout hit again. How is that even possible? I was putting into practice everything I had learnt. I was taking my meds. I was working flexibly. That sad little episode was behind me; I had a job to do, bills to pay, a family to provide for. Colleagues, however, became increasingly concerned about my health. It had become that obvious. My acting skills to portray a guy in control and on top of things clearly were not Oscar winning material. Then one sunny day in May, I was on a phone call with my manager, whilst working from home. We were discussing the huge projects and responsibilities I was delivering when suddenly … I stopped. The line went silent. I was rooted to the spot – again - and finally all I could say, before a tsunami of emotion hit me, was:

"I don't think I'm very well".

That was it. My last words to my manager and in fact the last moment I physically did any work for that company and industry again. The last time I had an employer, a manager, and what I'd describe as a job. Everything changed from that moment. Everything. This was worse; much worse than my first burnout. The outcome was being signed off from work. Unable to work.

Not for a few days, not a week, not even a month. One year.

The reality was that at the one year point I still had a very long way to go, but I needed to make a crucial decision about my future:

Do I return to the job, company and industry I knew so well? Or, do I politely leave that part of my life behind and face an even more uncertain future?

The year that changed everything

To understand the decision I made, we need to explore that one year of being signed off, unable to work. For, it was that year when the stark reality hit me - of the devastating and crippling consequences I was paying for years of living with worry, stress, anxiety, exhaustion and fear. I became unable to leave the house without severe anxiety. I was terrified of meeting or speaking to anyone, including my own loving family.

Insomnia greeted me every night, exhausting me mentally and physically. Heart-breaking paranoia consumed me, affecting my once stable relationships. I found comfort in self-isolation but leaving me alone with my thoughts was dangerous. The constant screaming voices in my head; those critical, loathing, vicious, vile, hateful inner voices. Tom Bilyeu in his motivational talk called "Self-Worth" says "No-one will ever hate you with the intensity that you can hate yourself." I know this to be undeniable truth and as a result, self-harm became the norm, as both punishment for being such a pathetic failure and to, in some way, release the pain.

In one last ditch attempt to shock me out of this dark hole I summoned everything I had, to go on a family vacation. To our favourite place on earth, with my whole loving family. This would work. It had to work. If this didn't have some sort of positive effect, nothing would. There's a certain irony to this giddy optimism during such a dark time. Giddy optimism is good – never lose that. Unfortunately, on this occasion, that wasn't enough.

The vacation was sprinkled with positives, but unsurprisingly in hindsight, it was physically, mentally and emotionally exhausting. It was sensory overload, which built until 19th August 2016. That's when it happened. After months of torment, spiralling into despair, trying but in my mind failing miserably, I made the ultimate decision. I believed I'd done all that could be done – I was on medication, I had been on the courses, I was away from work, I had a loving family, I had a change of scene; but, all hope was lost. I could no longer physically and mentally cope or be the burden I believed I was for those that I loved. I couldn't work. I could barely look after myself, let alone positively contribute to my relationships and family. I loved my family so much. I needed to release them; and myself.

The ultimate decision I made, was to end, my, life.

Let's take a breath

Let's take a moment, because, to be honest, that escalated quickly. You may in fact, want to note that as an important insight: things, important things, life changing, life ending things can escalate quickly. The journey may have been long, but the final sprint can be devastatingly quick. So, how on earth have we reached a point where the unspeakable, the unimaginable, the total opposite of life becomes the reality so desperately wanted? How?

Let's reflect on how we got here. Who has been the central character of our story? Conscientious. Down to earth. Fun. Social. Family loving. Working up the corporate ladder in a job and industry they kind of fell into. Doing the job, delivering the results. Paying the bills. Yes; that sounds like millions of people across the globe. So, what else?

Didn't like to let people down. Strong work ethic. Often took on more responsibility to demonstrate they were more than capable – and to avoid being cut in the next restructure. Worked increasingly long hours, both in the office and at home, thanks to our friend - technology.

Again, that sounds like millions of people across the globe. There must surely be something about this person that's so unique, so fascinating, or traumatic that makes this story make sense; because your everyday, down to earth, loving husband, father and employee just doesn't make that kind of ultimate decision.

Let's delve deeper. How about: Fearful of making mistakes. Fearful they didn't fit in. Fearful they'd be found out to be incompetent in some totally unrealistic way. Fearful of saying "No". Fearful of putting themselves first. Fearful of even putting their family first. Fearful of losing their job, their house, their marriage, their children. Fearful of failing. Fearful of not being good enough.

I'd love to be able to say: "There it is! There's the thing that makes this self-destructive tale make sense. That's why this person is not like everyone else; because normal (whatever that means) everyday people do not travel that path." I'd love to be able to say that; in fact, I wish, with all my heart, that I could say that. The painful truth, however, and it's a truth you may now have realised, is that there was nothing outstandingly different about this person. They had a normal, ordinary, life. A friendly, family orientated, working life. Just trying to do the best they could with the cards that life had dealt them.

This person is me, it's you, it's a family member, a friend, a neighbour, a colleague, a stranger. This person, in fact, is far too many of us. Far too many.

My story is our story
That's why, I believe, this story is so important to tell. That's why I need to be courageous and share my story with you. That's why I now dedicate my life to helping others, so they don't travel the same path I did … because this story is not just my story. It is the story of millions of hard working, wonderful people all over the planet; but too many do not live to tell their story. Too many, who do survive, have been through so much they don't recover … and way too many - millions upon millions - are working longer and harder for reasons they think are beyond question, and do not realise the path they are on.

Whether I was lucky, or the Universe had this plan for me all along, I don't know. What I do know though is I'm not squandering this second chance; and that's the realisation I had after my ultimate decision was unexpectedly, but gratefully, interrupted and foiled. All it took was an off guard answer to a reasonable question posed by my wife.

A little big conversation
My wife turned to me, with a worried look on her face.

"What's wrong? What are you thinking?"

There was a moment's pause, a deep breath; then I told her … everything. How I was feeling. How I couldn't cope anymore. How much I loved her, our children and family. How I couldn't think of any other way to stop the incessant pain inside and the burden I had become. I told her of my ultimate decision.

My best friend, soulmate, lover, wife. The woman who has been with me like a guardian angel since nursery school, when I would cruise around the church yard looking cool on my plastic red tractor!

It's by far, without a shadow of a doubt, the most heart breaking, courageous and important conversation I have ever had. It saved my life.

She saved my life. Calmly, sensitively, patiently, lovingly she changed my path.

It took a few years for my wife to open-up to me about what she was thinking in that moment; and it still makes me smile. My wife was relieved! Relieved I was going to end it all! My face must have been a picture when she told me that. I certainly didn't recall my wife letting out a hearty "phew, for a moment Martin I thought it was something important!".

What she meant by this though, was quite remarkable. She was relieved because she thought I wanted to leave her and get a divorce. In my incredible wife's mind, not loving her anymore and wanting a divorce was as bad as it could get. My ultimate decision was still just a decision. Despite my meticulous planning, I hadn't done it yet. I was still here; and for as long as that remained the case this was, in her words, "something we could get through together". What a truly remarkable woman.

There's a misconception about people wanting to take their own life – that it's in some way selfish, that they don't consider others, that they have no love left. That couldn't be further from the truth for most souls in this desperate moment. The decision is made for others. It's because we love them; because we feel we can no longer contribute in any meaningful way to our family. We are a burden; and remember, we are often very unwell.

So, continuing our story, with our love very much intact, my wife ensured I went straight to my doctor. My doctor, another remarkable woman, ensured I went straight to a higher level of therapy and to a psychiatrist. Now, whilst I was reluctant, if I'm honest, I had to admit this was something new. So, it did prove that I hadn't tried everything; and that's a lesson I carry with me every day.

Then the magic started

The first magical, enlightening moment was a further diagnosis. No longer "severe depression and high anxiety"; my Psychiatrist diagnosed me with "severe depression", and something called Generalised Anxiety Disorder. I remember saying: "Well I know what the anxiety part is, but I don't have a clue what the rest means!"

If anything, I thought it down-played the severity of it. Something "general" surely meant everyone has it, so just get on with it. Words are important, if you remember. This, however, wasn't just a fancy name for what we already knew. Not at all, this was something on a whole new level. This was a critical missing piece of my jigsaw puzzle that we didn't know existed until now. It certainly explained a lot.

My definition of Generalised Anxiety Disorder is that your brain is constantly in what's known as "Fight or Flight" mode. It essentially treats everything as a threat. Fight or Flight is the body's automatic reaction to danger. You are flooded with adrenaline, your senses are heightened, and you are preparing to either fight or run away from the huge, scraggly and very hungry looking sabre-toothed tiger standing right in front of you. Its teeth are huge, it can run very fast and you look like a tasty snack, despite the furry loin cloth you are wearing and the sturdy wooden club you have in your hand. This is truly a heart pounding encounter. This natural response is usually only sustainable, even for our club wielding friend, for a short period of time; 30 minutes or so. It puts so much strain on the body, it's exhausting. This is also essentially what happens during a panic or anxiety attack, which is why you can't keep still and are exhausted afterwards.

I use our cave dwelling friend as an example because this is how human beings are and always have been programmed. It's fascinating really and designed purely to keep us alive. Nowadays, however, we encounter less sabre-toothed tigers; but you will feel it kick in on a busy and slightly distracted Monday morning when you inadvertently step off the pavement when a bus is approaching. Did you feel the tightness in your chest as you visualised that?

So, what's all this cave dwelling, bus fuelled business got to do with Generalised Anxiety Disorder? Well, it means I'm constantly ready to fight or run from today's four wheeled sabre-toothed tigers. That's sensory, emotional, physical and mental overload. Always. Every second, of every minute, of every day. The screaming voices, the internal pressure, the pounding heart, the sick feeling, the shaking … Generalised Anxiety Disorder.

"Aha!" I hear you cry! "That's it! That's what is different and unique about you, Martin! You had this anxiety condition thing. All those millions of conscientious, hard-working, wonderful people around the world can breathe a sigh of relief!"

It's a fair observation; but, before you move on slightly disappointedly and somewhat relieved, you need to ask me a question. You need to ask me how you get Generalised Anxiety Disorder? Go ahead, ask me now. Say it out loud if it helps.

"Martin, how do you get Generalised Anxiety Disorder?"

What a great question! Thank you. I'm so glad you asked! Allow me to give you a simple, short answer … "Prolonged. Periods. Of Extreme. Stress."

In my case, years. All those years working longer and harder, constantly wired into work pressures and deadlines, not being able to sleep properly because I was thinking about work, unable to switch off at home to spend quality time with my wife and children, constantly on edge, irritable, frustrated … I don't think I need to go on.

This is part of the path. This is what it leads to. This is what will try to break you. This is what so nearly broke me. So, I am very much still concerned about those millions of conscientious, hard- working, wonderful people around the world; and this is yet another part of my story that is so important to share.

There's a cure though, right? That would be a reasonable assumption to make today. I am confident that a whole host of well qualified "experts", with or without experience of Generalised Anxiety Disorder, could debate this question. Personally, all I can tell you is, I still live with it; but there's a huge difference between being able to live with something and that something running every aspect of your life.

There is a powerful medication that can bring the anxiety levels down to normal-ish levels – and as soon as I was on that, it almost instantly enabled me to function and clear my head in a way I realised I hadn't experienced for a very long time. This is the important thing to understand about medication for depression and anxiety. It's not evil; and it's also not a cure. They allow you to have a clearer head; and a clearer head means healthier thoughts, feelings and actions. You can effectively put into place all the knowledge and strategies you've learnt. For me, that was the moment when my life and future finally felt positive again.

Finding myself

Therapy followed soon after and in one session we were discussing core beliefs and core values. The revelation that followed was life changing and life affirming. I stood up in the art room where this session was being held. Among the paint pots and brushes I was suddenly vividly aware of a dark, shadowy figure in the corner of my eye. I could feel the suppression intensely and I somehow knew it had been there for years, but it was as if once I saw it, catching it in the act of bringing me down, it slowly melted away. Then, for the first time in 20 years I felt like I'd rediscovered my true self once more. Content and confident in who I was, knowing full well that I was certainly good enough and with a clarity of purpose I'd never experienced before. I finally knew why I had been through everything I had endured. I finally knew why the people around me had always been there. I finally knew my purpose, my passionate purpose that embodied my entire body and soul:

I need to share my story with the world to help as many hard working, conscientious, wonderful people avoid the path I travelled, and so very nearly didn't survive. My entire life suddenly made sense. I was complete.

A message for you

If you see yourself or someone you care about in the early part of my anxiety story then: "Hi, I'm Martin and I share my story with you to bring you strength and encouragement. Life may feel tough, you may be dealing with the daily suppression of anxiety and overwhelm. It may feel like you're trapped and you're losing yourself in a vicious cycle of working harder and longer. Let my story, however, fuel your courage to seek new views, new ideas and new actions that can carve a new path; one that is more balanced and more joyful for you."

If you have struggled with the path I have travelled and survived. If you are my brothers and sisters on the same path as I am on right now, trying to make sense of your place in the world after such trauma: "Hi, I'm Martin and I share my story as a beacon of hope for You. You are good enough. You are courageous. You have an unrivalled strength. You have an incredible story that can inspire and save others. Your past can be used for good, but it doesn't define you."

If you are a loved one of someone who has or is struggling: "Hi, I'm Martin and you, my friend, are a Guardian Angel, just like my wife. I know how difficult it is. I know how irrational things can get. I know how desperately you want to help and heal. It's okay to not know what to say or do in every moment. Your love, your time, your patience, your touch are rays of sunshine upon a darkened but not yet lost soul. Keep talking, keep loving and keep the faith."

Reflection on our journey

As our story comes to an end, I thank you for being my companion on this journey. It has been a perilous but hopeful journey. Much has been learnt and there is still much to reflect on. My renewed perspective on life affords me the privilege to truly appreciate what a miracle life is. The trillions of things, across billions of years that needed to align for you and me to be here right now on this beautiful planet are just staggering. It's, therefore, worth every effort to embrace this precious gift of life we've been given. We don't get to decide what challenges we face in life; but we do get to decide how we react to them. Something we often forget is that we always have a choice. Always. I don't pretend that all choices are easy; many are far from that. They often require courage, strength and faith. The courage and strength to reach out – to trust that there is always a conversation you haven't had, that there is always a person you haven't spoken to and that there is always something you haven't tried. The faith that things can and will work out - that the struggle, the hardship will be worth it. One of the best things you can do is to stop, step back and start making healthy choices. You can emerge victorious, wiser, proud and with a level of gratitude and love second to none. I know this to be true, just as I know you are good enough; and your anxiety is NOT the tax you have to pay for the privilege of living and working in the 21 st Century.

In your life's journey and that of your loved ones, I wish you all the courage and strength needed to rise above the systems and processes, the environments and cultures, the expectations and judgements of others and stand confidently as the "Author and Hero of Your Life Story".

About Martin Seville

With a successful 20-year corporate career, life seemed good. Behind the smile and the sunglasses, however, there was a battle with debilitating, life-threatening mental illness, caused by years of built-up stress and anxiety. From this trauma, however, Martin discovered his Life Purpose. He now coaches, mentors, teaches and inspires from the stage as many people as he can, to improve their current quality of life and avoid the dark paths he travelled. After all, life is for living, not just existing.

He shares his story in support of and to raise awareness of the millions of hard working, conscientious people around the globe who are suffering in silence, and who so desperately need to know there is another way.

Martin describes his Mission as Becoming the Hero of Your Life Story. www.martinseville.com

Martin dedicates this chapter to his Guardian Angel wife, Emma, his wonderful boys, all the incredible professionals, family and friends that supported him through his darkest times and all those touched by what starts as stress and anxiety.

The Medicine Of The Future Is Sound
by Anne Phey

The psychic Edgar Cayce predicted that "The medicine of the future is sound". We have definitely already stepped into this future.

Sound is being used in medicine, such as ultrasound machines who can create images of our body and used to reduce kidney stones. Sound frequency is also being used by physiotherapists and chiropractors to heal muscles and align the spine. Allopathy use sound to ease pain and stress. Psychologists and psychotherapists use music to induce clam and reduce anxiety. Learning disability therapists use stimulating sounds to assist children to learn better. Holistic therapists use Tibetan metal and Crystal quartz singing bowls to create a sense of calm and relaxation.

There are good sounds & there are sounds that are not so pleasing to the ears or beneficial to our well-being. In the eagerness to get onto the sound healing trend, some practitioners just purchase a singing bowl or drum and start calling themselves sound therapists without the appropriate training. I have sat in sessions where well known musician turned sound therapists have created more dissonant cacophony than deep positive healing sound. As such, I have spent the past years since 2015 sharing about sound therapy to provide some insights into what is truly the power of sound healing.

My Journey In Sound

As a child, I was very sensitive to sound. I could feel the vibration of the weather changes in my body, and would run to tell my mum that it was going to rain. She didn't believe me initially, laughing if I was like a bird or dog, whose senses were more keen than humans. But time after time, the rain fall proved to her that her daughter had an accurate sensing.

Naturally, I picked up music, singing in the choir, playing the piano, performing violin solos and in the orchestra. Music continued to be a part of my life, playing for the church services, choir, gatherings and even had our own band of musicians. I loved music so much I worked for MTV (Music Television Network) Asia to promote local and overseas artists in Asia, Europe and the Americas.

A chance visit to Israel awakened a deep sense of passion to step beyond my corporate job to be of service to the community. I asked God what can I offer and the moment I returned home, the words "singing bowls" came to mind.

At that time, I did not know what that was. I opened up Facebook and an ad popped up on a Tibetan Singing Bowl workshop for that weekend. I took it as a sign from the universe and that began my sound healing journey.

Since 2015, I have trained in and taught certification programs for Tibetan metal and crystal singing bowls for beginners to practitioners. I also teach how to use our voice for sound healing and have produced two music albums to date.

When I conduct many one on one and group workshops, I witness how sound vibrational therapy supports the natural vibration of the body in aiding healing. These included physical reduction of dis-ease in the muscles, nerves, digestive, respiratory, reproductive, circulatory, emotional and mental states, including anxiety.

The Universe Is Sound!

Deepak Chopra, M.D. a medical visionary says "The Universe is sound!".

In the Old Testament's Book of Genesis on God, Hindu Vedic text on Brahman, ancient Egyptian writings on Thoth and Mayan on Popol Vuh - God was the word and the word was God, and the universe was created by the spoken word. So the world was created from sound.

Sound moves through the air in a wave measured in cycles per second, or Hertz (Hz). The measurement of sound is "frequency". Most humans can hear sounds up to 16,000 Hz while dolphins can hear up to 180,000 Hz. So while we cannot hear some sounds, we can feel their vibration. Even if we cannot feel the vibration, it exists.

Everything is vibration

Modern Physics shows that every smallest atom is in constant vibration. Every living and non-living thing vibrates at different rates. Everything in the universe is energy. Every matter, thought, belief, emotion, body and mind has its energy.

Our body is made up of different parts that vibrate in a different frequency. In 1992, Bruce Tainio built the first frequency monitor and determined that overall, a healthy body vibrates at a frequency of 62 to 72 MHz. When the frequency drops, the immune system is compromised. Lower vibration is associated with poor health, negative emotions and lack of consciousness.

Colds and flu starts at 57-60 MHz, Disease start at 58 MHz, Receptiveness to cancer at 42 MHz and Death at 25 MHz.

Besides the physical body and health, our emotional well-being also vibrates at different frequency. According to David R. Hawkins, the average person has a consciousness scale from Contracted Consciousness (such as shame at 20 Hz) to Ultimate Consciousness (such as enlightment at 700+ Hz). Within that scale, Peace vibrates at 600 Hz, Love at 500 Hz, Neutrality at 250 Hz, Anger at 150 MHz, Anxiety and Fear at 100 Hz.

What is Anxiety?

From an energy and vibration standpoint, anxiety is the anticipation of a future outcome underscored with uncertainty. It is self-doubt, worry when one cannot seem to control the outcome of the situation one is in.

For example, one can be anxious during a job interview as one wants to present the best self and becomes nervous. Another example is being anxious about one's image or afraid of making a mistake. Or one may be anxious in a place where one's safety may be at stake. Yet another example can be the fear of losing a relationship when certain conditions are not met, such as the other person not replying a message or being late.

As a result, one may not speak up, avoid or confront to keep the relationship. The subconscious mind repeats the incidences and feelings, so much so that when one is in a similar situation, the same feeling emerges. Sometimes, a small trigger can ignite the anxiety again.

Sound And Emotions In The Body

Many people feel emotions in different parts of the body. The reason is that different parts of the body vibrates to a different frequency. When the body experience a discomfort, it is due to that part of the body that falls below their usual frequency.

"Emotional feelings are associated with discrete, yet partially overlapping maps of bodily sensations, which could be at the core of the emotional experiences. Perception of these emotion-triggered bodily changes may play a key role in generating consciously felt emotions." as reported by the Proceedings of the National Academy of Sciences.

According to the Body Atlas produced from research conducted by Finnish scientist Lauri Nummenmaa from Aalto University in Greater Helsinki, our bodies expect different emotions to manifest in different parts. People with depression or anxiety often experience a pain in the chest. The body's stress response releases cortisol and hormones causing the person to react. Anxiety is commonly accompanied by fear which consumed the chest.

In the Body Atlas, anxiety shows up on the heat map mainly from the chest area and radiates upwards towards the head and downwards towards our gut. That is why in an anxiety attack, one often feels a tightening in the chest, difficulties in breathing, inability to speak, headaches and migraines or butterflies in the abdomen.

If we can identify where the body is feeling the sensation, we can use sound to alleviate the condition to bring about relief.

What Is The Impact Of Sound?

The power of sound is demonstrated in the work of Japanese scientist Dr Masaru Emoto on "Messages from Water".

In his first experiment, he played different music to see the effects of sound on water. Classical and new age music created extraordinary beautiful snow-flake shapes in the water crystals while heavy metal music created mud-like images.

In his second experiment, he used words such as "love" and "sick" on water. That too reflected the same snow-flake and muddy images respectively.

In his third experiment, he took polluted water from Fujiwara Dam in Japan that had a muddy structure and had a priest chant prayers over it for an hour. The water changed into snowflake structure again.

These experiments show how good sound, be it music, words or prayer, can affect water structure. If our body is made up of more than 70% water, imagine the impact of sound on our body's health.

It is the ability of consciousness encoded in sound waves that is the phenomenon of sound healing.

Types of Sound Healing

There are many types of sound healing you can explore to support your anxiety. Here are some common ones:

1. Words in Mantra, Chants, Prayers and Affirmations

Just like Dr Emoto's experiment, words have power to create beautiful snow-flake crystal shapes in water. We too can speak positive words to our water and drink it. We can also speak mantras, chants, prayers or affirmations to ourselves. The words will create a positive sound vibrational ripple through our entire being to bring it to wholeness.

See practice 1 which you can do on a daily basis to sharpen listening to create conscious awareness and speak positive affirmations to the areas we need in our various bodies.

2. Voice Toning

Our voice is one of the most powerful instrument. Voice toning by humming vowels that correspond to our body various vibrational frequency will bring it to balance.

See practice 2 where we use specific vowels that lifts the vibrational frequency of the three chakra areas most affected by anxiety – throat, heart and solar plexus.

3. Tibetan Metal Singing Bowls

Tibetan metal singing bowls have been used since ancient times in ordinary households for cooking, eating and healing. This lost art has now found its way to India and Nepal and to the world.

I practice and teach the Tibetan style of singing bowls where the sound is gentle and the vibrations are deep. Only use bowls that are old and hand-made as they offer a more mature and deep resonance. They can be used to hold sound baths where the sounds from these bowls are like waves that wash over our body and senses, immersing us in a calm ambience.

Each singing bowl when played, emits at least three to six different tones, creating sound waves that balances both the left and right hemisphere of the brains. This reduces brain-wave activity and induces states of relaxation.

Ancient or old bowls can be used for on body treatments. A certified practitioner can use these bowls placed on the physical body to allow the vibration to penetrate the muscles, nerves and organs to create deep relaxation and support the body to heal naturally. It also deepens the healing of the spiritual, etheric and emotional body. Specific placements and methods support anxiety alleviation.

Do not use store bought machine made bowls as they do not produce the harmonic sound frequency and can be jarring to the ears. Sounds that do not rest well affects the body's harmony. If you visit a sound practitioner, pay attention to their instruments to ensure they are of handmade quality. Also check in that the sound therapist is not striking the bowls like drums or cymbals, as that creates shock waves through the body.

Tingshas or cymbals are also used as part of the sound bath and for space clearing.

Recently, gongs have also become popular. The vibration from gongs are very powerful given their size and effect. Likewise, go for a gong sound bath only with reputable practitioners who have been trained to create positive resonance.

4. Crystal Singing Bowls

Crystal singing bowls were created in the last twenty years as the modern versions of the Tibetan metal bowls. They are made from silica quartz. Some producers of crystal bowls add other crystal powders to create different colours and vibrations. Different crystals have different vibrational properties. So crystal bowls with different crystals infused will impart properties of those crystals. For example, a rose quartz crystal bowl will add on the vibrations of love and softness to the sound therapy.

The sound is similar to rubbing the edge of the wine glass to produce a sound. Crystal bowls are often used in sound baths. Their sounds are more singular and focused compared to the more harmonic Tibetan singing bowls. Some people resonate more with Tibetan and some with crystal singing bowls. It is a matter of preference.

5. Tuning Fork Therapy

This modality of sound healing was pioneered by Dr John Beaulieu. Tuning forks are designed to specific frequencies. During the process, the body aligns with the interval created by the tuning forks, balancing the nervous system.

Sonopuncture is using sound as acupuncture "needles" to work on the traditional Chinese systems of meridian medicine.

6. Singing and Music Therapy

Since history, songs have been used to boost morale in battles, create excitement, soothe the heart in romance, and create relaxation. Music therapy is often used in spas, treatments by practitioners and played by many via radio, CDs and online music.

Listening to soothing music is one way to release anxiety. There are many options:

(a) 432Hz music which resonates closely to nature and allows the body to come into a relaxed state.

(b) Binaural beats are now popular although there isn't much scientific proof that it works. I know it works because one of my music album was created with binaural beats and when my partner was listening to it while talking to someone, fell asleep mid conversation! Binaural beats in the alpha frequencies (8 to 13 Hz) encourages relaxation, promote positivity, and decrease anxiety. Binaural beats in the theta (4 to 8 Hz) range are linked to REM sleep, reduced anxiety, relaxation, as well as meditative and creative states.

(c) Classical music were used by many mothers during their pregnancies to create clever babies. If you enjoy classical music, you may find this option suitable for you. Or whatever makes you relax.

(d) Sounds of Nature

Many who suffer from anxiety and insomnia find that listening to nature soothing and are better able to be calm and fall asleep. Examples include sounds of rain, sea waves, birds.

Self-Practice

Here are two practices that you can do on your own.

Practice 1: Mindful Listening & Sound Healing With Words

Hearing is the first and last sense that we come into this world and leave it by. Just by focusing on our hearing, we can pick up sounds from a far distance and be able to perceive our world.

This is a practice for those who are comfortable with silence. If for any reason, you are not comfortable with silence, try the other exercise listed in this chapter.

Find a relatively quiet place where you will not be disturbed.

Sit comfortably and observe your surroundings.

Then close your eyes and be as still as you can. For those who are uncomfortable closing your eyes, you can try to lower your gaze instead.

Be aware of your breath. Listen to your breath.

As you become more still and quiet, the more conscious you will be of the sounds around you.

Now use your hearing to sense your surroundings (just like you did with your eyes earlier, but with your ears).

What do you hear? Perhaps the ticking of the clock or watch, the swirl of the fan, the hum of the refrigerator, or the start & stop of the air-conditioner from time to time.

Now use your hearing to explore beyond your immediate surroundings to the outside environment.

What do you hear? Perhaps the neighbour's TV program, conversations, children laughing, dogs barking in the distant, traffic of the vehicles on the road, the whisper of the wind?

How is this different from when you were just using your eyes? Perhaps you can hear more than what you could see?

Are you able to visualize or feel the energy of what you are hearing?

Now bring your awareness back to yourself and the space you are sitting in.

Focus on and listen to your breath. Allow all the other sounds to fade away.

Breathe as deeply and as slowly as you can.

As you continue to breathe deeply, listen to your body.

Your body may respond back in sound. Perhaps a throaty breath in the neck area, a wheezing in your windpipe, the beating of the heart, a rumbling in your stomach or a crackling of your joint.

Your body may also respond in other ways, such as a knowing, feeling, sense or hunch. Perhaps tension in your shoulders, a dull ache in the back, butterflies in your tummy, or a grounded connection to Mother Earth.

Don't worry if you are not able to hear anything. Just focus on your breath on each inhalation and exhalation.

Specifically for anxiety

If you sense any pre-existing or arising anxiety, acknowledge it by saying "I sense anxiety". If you sense any other emotions at the same time, you can also name those, "I sense anxiety, fear and anger."

Breathe deeply and sense which part of the body is feeling it. If you are able to sense that, acknowledge it by saying "I sense anxiety (and other named emotions) in my chest, (any area of the body you sense, such as stomach, throat, head etc). "

If you are not able to sense which specific part of the body, just say "I sense anxiety in my body".

Now breathe deeply into that area of the body with strong intention and say "I release anxiety from my body (or name the areas of the body)".

Now breathe deeply into that area again and visualize the anxiety leaving in faith. Faith is believing the unseen. Our intention and faith is important to support the healing.

If instead of anxiety, you are experiencing any other physical or emotional discomfort, you can also do the same by naming the discomfort and the area of the body, and then breathing to alleviate the discomfort.

Take another deep breath and say a prayer of gratitude for our ability to breathe, see, hear and be alive.

When you are ready, gently open your eyes with a big smile.

This exercise is a great way to centre and ground yourself, be present and still. It works well for those with anxiety to observe without responding or reacting.

The combination of listening and sensing, breathing and speaking to the areas of discomfort is a way to send the vibrational frequency using words and sound to alleviate the dis-ease.

If you enjoyed this exercise, you can do it and shift your focus on the sounds nearest to you to those furthest to you. The more you practice, the more acute your sense of hearing will be. This exercise also trains us to be aware of what's external and creates a calm space from which we can view the world. Imagine if we have this calm state, we are in a better position to face our daily challenges. Practising this daily will create an internal defence mechanism to alleviate anxiety.

Practice 2: Voice Healing

Find a place where you can make sounds and not be disturbed.

Sit comfortably and keep your back straight and yet relaxed.

Then close your eyes and be as still as you can. For those are uncomfortable closing your eyes, you can try to lower your gaze instead.

Be aware of your breath and your body.

Listen to your breath and your body. (To practice listening to your body, refer to practice 1.)

Part a: Solar Plexus Chakra

Now focus on the abdomen area, a little above the navel or belly button. This is where the Solar Plexus chakra is located. This chakra works with the digestive organs. This is where we hold our power centre and feel confident. When one experiences anxiety, one can sometimes lose our confidence and experience nervousness in this area.

Open your mouth gently and softly make the sound of the vowel "OH" (as in "go"). Allow it to be in the middle of your comfortable range, not too high.

Focus on your attention on your Solar Plexus chakra at the navel and project the sound there. As you continue to hum the vowel, allow the sound to saturate the entire area from inside out.

As you do so, experience this centre becoming balanced and healthy.

Repeat this seven times or until you feel the pain or congestion diminishing, and the anxiety reducing.

Part b: Heart Chakra

Begin by focusing on the middle of your chest area. This is where the heart chakra is located. The heart chakra works with the heart and lungs. This is where one feel the emotions of love, mercy and compassion. When one is off balance, this is where anxiety is often experienced.

Open your mouth gently and softly make the sound of the vowel "AH" (as in "ma"). Allow it to be in the middle of your comfortable range, not too high or low. Let it be a little higher than the tone used at the navel area.

Focus on your attention on your heart chakra and project the sound there. As you continue to hum the vowel, allow the sound to saturate the entire area from inside out.

As you do so, experience this centre becoming balanced and aligned to the previous chakra.

Repeat this seven times or until you feel the pain or congestion diminishing, and the anxiety reducing.

Part c: Throat Chakra

Next, focus on the throat area. This is where the Throat chakra is located. This chakra works with your communication organs, including the ears for hearing and the voice for speaking.

When one experiences anxiety, it can lead to an inability to hear or voice out.

Open your mouth gently and softly make the sound of the vowel "Eye" (as in "my"). Allow it to be in the middle of your comfortable range, a little higher than the tone you used for the heart chakra.

Focus on your attention on your throat area and project the sound there. As you continue to hum the vowel, allow the sound to saturate the entire area from inside out.

As you do so, experience this centre becoming balanced and aligned to the heart chakra, which is aligned to the Solar Plexus.

Repeat this seven times or until you feel the pain or congestion diminishing, and the anxiety reducing.

Closing gratitude prayer

Take a deep breath and say a prayer of gratitude or appreciation for our ability to breathe, speak, hear, feel and be alive.

When you are ready, gently open your eyes with a big smile.

Make Sound A Daily Support For Anxiety

Now that we understand that we need to vibrate at 62 to 72 Hz for good health and above 250 Hz for positive emotions, compared to 100 Hz for Anxiety. Sound therapy can be applied personally through good music and sound, our own voice using vowel toning or attending sound therapy sessions with certified professionals. Let's start with the two practices that I have shared and make a difference to shift into a healthier state of being.

About Anne Phey

Anne Phey is an International Coaching Federation Associate Certified Coach and a Holistic Practitioner, and the Founder of The Conscious Flow Pte Ltd. She has a Masters of Arts from the University of Singapore and a Masters of Business Administration (Strategic Change Management) from the University of Hull in United Kingdom.

Anne believes in bringing out the authentic self in all its beauty, to uncover the gifts and empower one to reach the highest potential and to make a difference in one's life.

As a highly accomplished professional, she is keenly aware of the corporate pressures and has helped many individuals discover their true self, find their purpose, harmonize their work life and develop their potentials in life.

She is gifted in the ancient mastery of love from the heart, generosity of spirit, spontaneity in connections and creativity in healing. Anne practices a wide range of modalities and creates her unique blend for each unique individual.

Anne Phey's life is devoted to helping others discover the divine bliss that is our birthright. Her gentle, warm guidance will enable us to uncover our true self, realize our hidden talents, overcome tribulations, heal and transform, and most importantly, live our lives to our true purpose. Her deep love for those whom she guides opens up pathways of consciousness and gently nurtures us towards our divine states. Anne is pioneering the path for next generation of mindful leaders and conscious businesses. To find out more, please visit: AnnePhey.com

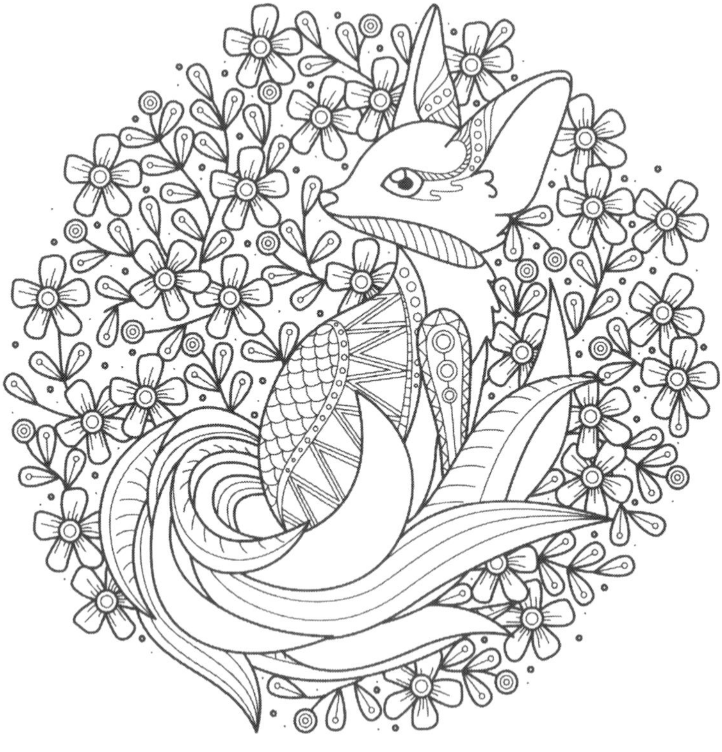

Be Your Own "Emotional Electrician" With Yoga.
by Sean J.W. Low

As a human resource manager and coach, I have observed a steady increase in the number of executives seeking help to manage stress and anxiety over the years. Based on a 2019 survey by healthcare consultancy firm Asia Care Group on behalf of health insurance and services company Cigna, 84% of survey respondents from around the world reported feeling stressed, with 64% stating that they felt the need to engage with work outside office hours. Closer to home in Singapore, it was estimated that the nation spent approximately US$2.3 billion or 18% of its annual total healthcare budget on stress-related illnesses such as hypertension, which was just slightly behind Australia's 18.8%. These are huge amounts.

As a working employee myself, I can understand how our modern work culture has become so frenetic. With the onslaught of information and requests 24/7 from multiple devices through emails, calls, social media, text messaging, work is no longer confined to a physical venue we call the office. Our working hours have increased and we spend a lot of time online and waiting for notifications from our devices. Sometimes, it can feel as if our mind and body react to pings from our mobile devices and deadlines as if our survival is at risk. With the multi-sensory overload of information and the hyper-vigilance we accord to our devices, it is no surprise that stress and anxiety have become prevalent conditions among employees.

Stress is not all bad. In fact, moderate stress can enhance our performance. Stress only becomes a problem when it turns into anxiety where stress responses are triggered for prolonged periods over threats that may not be realistic. Much like a race car that has gone into an overdrive longer than needed, our system can become worn down over time with prolonged stress responses. The ability to moderate stress and anxiety is thus important, and has been found to be important in encouraging productivity and performance.

I was intrigued by the ability of yoga to moderate stress and anxiety when I stumbled on this ancient practice while I was a student pursing my psychology degree. I found the practice empowering as it accords practical methods to the individual to work with the body, breath and mental attitudes to tame our stress responses during times of stress and anxiety. Under proper guidance and correct practice, it can even promote feelings of peace, contentment and gratitude. These are powerful emotions that have positive relationships with performance. I went on to pursue my yoga teacher training, and coupled the practice of yoga with wisdoms from other body-mind practices like Tai Chi and Pilates as well as my training in psychology, to help thousands of executives and employees cope with the stress and anxiety and empower them to be more effective in their work and life.

In the last decade, one of the most frequently posed questions to me is how I managed to guide others in a way that brings them effective results. To me, the answer is clear. It is certainly not about getting people into challenging poses like headstands or shoulder stands. My regular participants could testify that I hardly make them go into challenging postures. What I find important is understanding the underpinning principles of the field of body-mind as well as having a solid grasp on the growing scientific research in the field, and integrating the knowledge into the teaching. It is not just about "what" you ask people to do. As important is the "why" of what you ask people to do in the context of their condition, and "how" you guide people to do what they do. Often, the simpler the better. With this, I will start by elucidating the science of anxiety, which forms the principles on how I harness body-mind approaches to manage this condition. I hope that the knowledge will empower more people to better manage anxiety, and I am excited by the vision of a world where more people can tap on the knowledge to enhance productivity and harness more of our potential.

Our Nervous System and Anxiety

Our nervous system plays an important role in anxiety, and no remedy would be complete without an understanding on the relationship between the two. A balanced nervous system sees the two branches of the autonomic nervous system, which control the body's arousal and preparation for action, functioning in equilibrium. The sympathetic nervous system (SNS) branch or the fight-or-flight branch of the nervous system is designed to accelerate our gears when a threat is detected. It is like an emergency alarm in our system which raises our heart rate, respiration rate, blood pressure and stress hormones to prime our body for action to keep us safe from harm. When danger has passed, the parasympathetic nervous system (PNS) or the relax-and-digest branch of the nervous system kicks in to put a brake on the stress response so that we do not waste energy leaving the alarms ringing when there is no need to. It is like a mute switch that calms and conserves our energy by lowering our heart rate, breathing rate, blood pressure and stress hormones, strengthening our immune system and increasing digestion.

Both SNS and PNS function in synergy to enable us to respond appropriately to situations. Neither system is good or bad; the key is balance. The SNS enables us to respond to the demands of life; the PNS slows us down, conserves our energy and enables us to rest and relax. Anxiety occurs when we see a hyper-reactive SNS while the PNS is unable to slow things down as quickly, resulting in a fight-or-flight reaction each time.

Neuroplasticity Wires the Patterns of Anxiety

No matter how long we have been living with anxiety, it is vital to remember that we are born with the capacity for our SNS and PNS to function in balance. What we are feeling and experiencing in anxiety are due to the prolonged wiring of anxiety patterns into our system over time by a mechanism that scientists called neuroplasticity. This is what makes it hard to imagine that we can respond in any other way.

Neuroplasticity is the ability of our brain to alter and build connections among neurons in the brain. It is the mechanism that enables us to learn and transform with experiences so that responses to subsequent experiences can become more efficient. Neuroplasticity works through repetition. The repetition of particular thoughts, emotions or behaviours form associations and networks among neurons. These changes, albeit small at first, when repeated over time can create strong networks with a magnetic pull that compels us to think, feel and behave in particular ways that seem automatic and difficult to resist.

The root of anxiety is thus seeded long before we become aware of its effects. Each time we think an anxious thought, experience panic or engage in frenetic behaviours in response to a perceived threat in the environment, we stimulate corresponding groups of neurons in the brain. Over time, these different sensations, thoughts and emotions become linked into a pattern of anxiety. Each subsequent repetition of the pattern wires it more deeply into the system, changing our neural chemistry and wiring over time. When the links are strong, what happens in one part of the network can also trigger sensations in other parts, leading to a full-blown experience of the anxiety pattern. Our neuro system has learned too well how to trigger the full protective response with the slightest hint of a threat.

Neuroplasticity as the Solution to Anxiety

Just as neuroplasticity provides an explanation for anxiety, it can also provide a solution. Just as we can wire ourselves with patterns of anxiety, we can also re-wire ourselves with patterns of relaxation and balance. Remember that every repetition is an opportunity to leave a new trace in the brain and body. This entails accessing the PNS and strengthening the neural pathways to activate the system in times of stress. This is best done when we are not stirred up so that these connections can compete with the more reactive ones and be readily accessible to bring us back to balance in times of stress. Over time, we can exert greater mastery over our experiences by raising arousal levels when needed and turning them down when we need more calm.

A Body-Mind Approach in Managing Anxiety

Now that we have a better understanding on the science of anxiety, how can we apply the knowledge to build a practice that helps us manage the condition? I recommend developing and strengthening our new wiring through three categories of practices. Each category requires ongoing practice over time. The keyword here is time. While we may wish for instant change, this magic does not exist in reality. Knowing the science, the nervous system accommodates small increments of change through repetition. It is not set up to assimilate instant transformation. Any force to effect instant transformation will only aggravate the nervous system and put pressure on our body while we are trying to change. We need to have patience and compassion towards our body. With this patience, we can then reap the fruits of all three practices to help us muscle over the stress pathways in anxiety.

Work with Our Body to Develop Pathways to Balance and Relaxation

As we came to understand previously, the PNS or the relax-and-digest branch of the nervous system puts a brake on stress responses and brings us back to balance. To develop competitive wiring against more reactive responses, we need to develop and strengthen the pathways that activate the PNS in times of stress.

A key agent of the PNS is the vagus nerve, and 80 per cent of the vagus nerve fibers are afferent which means that these nerve fibers convey information from the body to the brain. This is good news as it suggests that any practice that stimulates the vagus nerve in the body can activate the PNS to bring us back to balance and relaxation in times of stress. With the vagus nerve running from the back of our head through to nearly all the thoracic and abdominal organs, nearly all the physical practices in yoga are capable of stimulating this nerve to trigger relaxation. These practices improve blood circulation in the body, activate the PNS and thus relax our body and the anxious mind.

So what are some specific physical practices that we can engage in to strengthen these pathways to the PNS? Knowing the hectic lifestyle of a working employee, I know that it will be hard to prescribe a practice that requires them to set aside time each day to practice yoga on a mat. Through the years of teaching and studying the physical practices of yoga, I have developed a set of practices that are effective in triggering relaxation among employees. The key of my approach is simplicity. These practices are simple, easily executed in office settings, and can be done without the need to change into workout gear. I cannot emphasise enough that we need to look past our assumption that only dramatic interventions can withstand the power of anxiety. As we understand from the science, the nervous system accommodates small increments of change through repetition, and simple practices of relaxation works well to support this change. I will share three such yoga-inspired practices. They are the modified forward bend, modified child's pose, and the modified twist.

a. Modified Forward Bend
- Sit on a chair.
- Set the feet comfortably on the floor.
- Inhale, and as we exhale, fold the body over the thigh.
- Hug the body from underneath the thigh with hands on opposite elbows.
- Allow the body weight to rest comfortably over the thigh.
- Slow our breathing in and out of the nose, and feel the stretch on the back.
- Stay in the stretch for at least eight breaths.

b. Modified Child's Pose
- Sit on a chair.
- Set both palms face down on the edge of the table at shoulder-width distance apart.

- Shift the chair backwards away from the table as far as possible with the palms still pressed on the table.
- As we have shifted our body, bring the feet position on the floor back towards the body with knee above the ankle.
- Inhale, and as we exhale, fold the body over the thigh with palms still pressing on the table.
- Slow our breathing in and out of the nose. Feel the stretch on the back and shoulders, and the grounding of the belly towards the thigh.
- Stay in the stretch for at least eight breaths.

c. Modified Twist
- Sit on a chair.
- Set the feet comfortably on the floor with both knees and thigh together.
- Bring the palms together in front of the body in a prayer position.
- Inhale, and as we exhale, take a twist and bring the right elbow to the outside of the left thigh.
- Draw the elbow at the top (i.e. left elbow) back and feel the stretch on the back and shoulders as we twist.

- Slow our breathing in and out of the nose, and stay for at least eight breaths.
- Repeat on the other side (i.e. twist with left elbow to the outside of the right thigh).

Work with Our Breath to Trigger Relaxation

Among the functions regulated by the autonomic nervous system, only breathing can be controlled consciously. Regulating the breath is integral to body-mind practices. Yoga believes that the breath and mind move in tandem. When the breath moves in a certain pattern, it triggers associated thoughts in the mind. When the mind moves in a certain way, the breath moves along with it. An anxious mind comes with short, shallow and rapid breathing; a relaxed mind comes with considerably slower, deeper breathing. If we are able to mimic the breathing patterns of balance and relaxation by deliberately slowing down our breath, we can induce a state of relaxation. This phenomenon has been validated by scientific studies which found that mimicking breathing patterns of particular emotional experience creates that experience. Practice this enough and we can strengthen the pathways that lead to balance and relaxation.

To trigger relaxation, the approach is to slow the breathing in and out through the nose, and aim for deep breathing right down to the abdominal area. Breathing this way stimulates the vagus nerve fibres that innervate the diaphragm, which triggers the PNS and sends a cascade of rest and relaxation responses throughout the body. When our breathing is slow and relaxed, our nervous system detects the message that we are safe and well and sends a cascade of changes in the body and mind to prevent or interrupt an emergency stress response. Regular practitioners of breath practice can also try to lengthen the exhalation to be at least twice as long as the inhalation for each breath. Lengthening the exhalation accentuates the calming effect on the nervous system and makes it even more effective in intercepting stress responses.

For us to feel the effects of breath work on our psychological state, I usually encourage anxious employees to stay with breath practice for at least ten minutes. Those who find this challenging due to a long-standing habit of breathing shallowly and rapidly can begin with eight breaths, working up to ten breaths, five minutes and then ten minutes over time. I will share the instructions that I typically use to guide employees to relaxation. I hope they will be helpful to guide you in your breath practice.

Guide for Breath Work for Relaxation

Be in a comfortable position – you can be in a sitting or lying down position.

Close your eyes and allow your whole body to relax. Turn your awareness inside your body and take a scan from head to toes. Get aware of whether you are holding on to any tension in the body. If you are, allow yourself to soften and let go.

With the awareness inside your body, turn your attention to the slow breathing in and out of the nose. Feel the slow flow of air in and out through your nostrils, the pause between the in-breath and the out-breath, and finally the flow of air out through the nostrils.

Once comfortable with breathing in and out through the nose, see if you can breathe even more deeply by letting the air reach right down to the abdomen area. Feel the belly rising with every in-breath, and the belly gently falling down with every out-breath.

With every breath that you take, see if you can slowly lengthen the out-breath to be at least twice as long as the in-breath.

Observe our Anxiety Patterns in a State of Calm

When we activate the PNS with the above body and breath exercises, we will find that we are able to observe our anxiety and the situation in a different psychological state. We are somehow able to observe the hysteria of the mind and the emotionally charged situation from a more detached vantage point, much like watching a thunderstorm from a sheltered room. This is why I sometimes guide anxious employees through a truncated version of the above exercises during coaching sessions when I observe that their thoughts are cluttered with stress responses. The exercises almost certainly ground them in the present moment and enable them to observe the situation from a more neutral perspective.

With an interlude of not being anxious, we have the opportunity to identify the patterns that trigger our anxiety and enable us to reframe situations as less stressful e.g. "I'm only late for the meeting; I am not going to die", "My boss is having a bad day; it has nothing to do with me". This can heighten our awareness of the stories in our head that filter our experience of the situation that cause us anxiety, and empower us to make different choices rather than settling for the default responses. This also opens up a gap for healthier patterns to form and take root.

Developing awareness of the patterns that root us in anxiety is the most challenging aspect of the three practices in my opinion. With the discomfort and pain that comes with anxiety, what I see often in employees who suffer from this condition is that they tend to run away from rather than inhabit the body and mind to examine the underlying patterns. They would rather turn to whatever distracts from the pain and discomfort such as external solutions of entertainment. But the more we run away, the less likely we are to become conscious of the thoughts, self-talk, feelings and actions that reinforce the patterns of anxiety. And if we keep rehearsing these patterns, how can we break out of them?

I recommend dedicating some ten minutes in silence after the body and breath practices to examine the patterns that trigger our anxiety such as the nature of our thoughts, self-talk and even our body movements. Are we dwelling in the future in a negative way? Are there alternative interpretations of the situation that we are missing? Is this thought or idea likely to happen? Were we engaging in fast movements such as fidgeting or pacing unnecessarily prior to the bout of anxiety? Being aware of our anxiety patterns enables us to recognise them the next time before full-fledged anxiety is triggered, and help us prevent further imprint onto the anxiety wiring.

Conclusion

The above three practices of working with our body, breath and awareness to develop and strengthen our pathways to balance and relaxation are best done before we are stirred up in emotionally stressful situations. I recommend consistent practice three times a week and 30 minutes each time (10 minutes each for the body, breath and awareness practice in that order) to build resilience to stress and anxiety before they occur.

In emergency situations when we feel symptoms of stress responses such as an elevated heart rate, sweating, quick and shallow breathing, we can also do an abridged version of the practices to quickly interrupt stress responses. I recently helped an employee who was suffering from anxiety due to the challenges he was facing in his personal life. I coached him into the modified forward bend, got him to stay in the stretch for eight rounds of breath, and guided him to practice eight rounds of slow and deep abdominal breathing in a relaxed sitting position. The following day, he shared with me that not only did he experience a significant reduction in his stress responses, he also had the best night sleep in a while!

I am truly excited by the scientific findings that we can be our own emotional electrician who can wire ourselves in healthier ways. And the tools offered by body-mind practices such as yoga can help wire us to balance and relaxation by stimulating the vagus nerve and activating the PNS. When we have lived with anxiety for some time, it is tempting to view our body and mind as a liability. It is important to remember the powerful healing system built within all of us that we can harness as a resource for healing through the practice of body, breath and awareness. What we need is patience and consistent practice to set the new wiring in place. By sharing this knowledge, I hope that it will empower more people to better manage anxiety so that we can bring more of our gifts to the world.

About Sean J.W. Low

Sean is a human resource manager in a technology organisation in Singapore and an ICF-certified coach. He is also trained as a yoga teacher. Sean is excited by the vision of a world where everyone can bring forth more of their gifts and potential. He aspires to empower individuals and organisations with tools and knowledge to recognise and harness their unique strengths and brilliance.

Having worked with many executives and employees over the years, Sean observed that there are several barriers standing in the way of employees maximising their productivity and potential. Anxiety is one of them. Having personally experienced positive changes to his responses towards stressful situations following his intensive 200 hours yoga teacher training, Sean firmly believes in the efficacy of body-mind practices in managing stress and anxiety. He has since brought the practice to thousands of employees. He is excited by the growing body of scientific evidence that supports the positive changes experienced by him and those he coached. To connect with Sean, please visit Facebook: www.facebook.com/sean.bodymindfitness or LinkedIn: www.linkedin.com/in/jinwei-sean-low

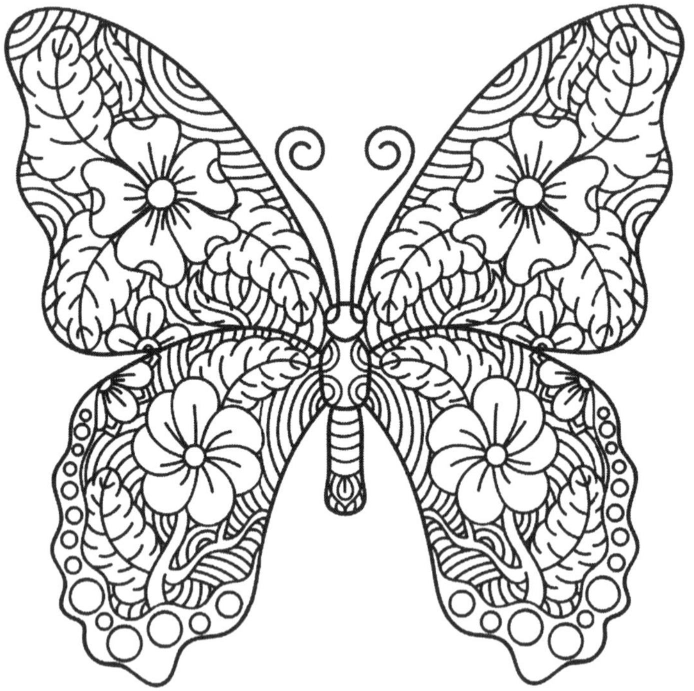

Youier, The Ultimate Happiness Hack!
by El Edwards

It was over a decade ago but I remember the moment like it was yesterday. The eye roll. The feeling of being squashed, constrained. I was lining up to enter my then three year old's school concert and had just launched into an animated story, complete with voices. I thought I was entertaining and based on the visual cues, my "audience" that day tended to agree but then I caught the eye roll from someone queuing alongside me. Apparently not everyone enjoyed my storytelling that day.

The message I heard loud and clear from that eye roll? "Be quiet! Stop making a spectacle of yourself. Stop sticking out and drawing such attention to yourself!" It was like someone had taken the very essence of my spirit, chucked it in a bottle and relegated it to the dustbin. It was rubbish to be the animated, story-telling me. I was rubbish. The only way to survive is to tone it down, be less. I guess it's no small coincidence that that was a time in my life when I was at my most miserable!

Over the last few chapters you've been introduced to things that you can do to help alleviate anxiety holistically but, thanks to that

eye roll back in 2005, for the next little while we're going explore anxiety from a slightly different angle ... happiness. Happiness isn't the polar opposite of anxiety but if we can help increase your day to day happiness it'll make it easier for you to apply the strategies and advice given in the other chapters of this book.
"Every day may not be wonderful, but there's something wonderful in every day." - Anon.

By learning to see the "something wonderful" around you, you can be happy right now today, even while you're struggling with anxiety and so my goal through this chapter is to give you some bits and pieces to play with, things that you can try that can give you that glimmer of happiness, to encourage and lift you.

One of the big pieces linked to happiness is a sense of purpose. You might have been told that if you find your "thing", your purpose, your reason for being on the planet, that you will be happy. Personally I'm not convinced! Sure, a sense of purpose is great but it's no guarantee of happiness. I learned this first hand ...

Back in 2009, my local church founded a charity called Give A Brick and early 2010, in a bid to raise the profile of the charity, I started blogging and hanging out on Twitter. I fell into the world of personal development and people earning money in their PJs. As a young mum of three, this idea was hugely appealing to me and so, after doing some business training that told me I needed to know my purpose in order to find ideal clients, I commenced a two year journey into "thing finding"

What's my purpose? What am I put on this planet to do? What, why, where - and lots of similar "big questions". It was incredibly stressful and led to an awful lot of anxiety so forgive me for being less than certain that "find your thing" leads to happiness!

Fast forward to mid-2012 and I gave up on "thing finding". It was just too stressful. I decided instead to simply be me. Now thankfully along the way I'd learnt some practical skills that I could apply whilst "being me", such that I swiftly built a rather successful virtual assistant business. Clients came to me via word of mouth. I never had to worry about marketing or competing with others. It was great!

Little did I know then that this "being me" thing would turn out to be the foundation of Youier By Design, the happiness work I share with people today, nearly a decade later. I should have seen it coming though. The contrast between my happiness levels when I was playing small back in 2005 versus "being me" in

2012 when suddenly everything just made sense? The difference is like night and day!

Youier, you being you, the person God made you to be, is the ultimate "secret" to day to day happiness but it doesn't happen by accident, hence why it's known as Youier By Design.

In the rest of this chapter, we'll be playing with the four main areas of Youier By Design: Goal setting, Productivity, Wellbeing & Faith. It won't be the ultimate guide to you being Youier. (That actually makes up a whole series of books!) Instead, each section will leave you with one practical plaything, plus the occasional link to places where you can find out more if you decide you'd like to go a little deeper in any of these four areas. So, with that said, let's jump straight in!

Youier Goal Setting

Goal setting is a bit like marmite, you either love it or hate it. And most people who fall into the latter camp do so because they got tired of wishing and hoping for the same things year after year and never seeing any progress!

As someone who used to live very firmly in that second camp, I feel your pain. The definition of insanity is doing the same thing over and over again and expecting different results so how about this time we play with setting goals you actually want to get done? One size does not fit all. Instead, I'm here to introduce you to a process that gives you the freedom to play with this your own way.

Let's start with an important reminder ... your "thing" is to be you, the person God created you to be. That's it. Period. End of.

And at the same time, you being you, there will be things that niggle at you. Dreams, ambitions, aspirations. Call them what you will, those things that niggle at you are God's hints at what "you being you" really looks like.

And that, ultimately, is why goal-setting is so important. Life moves fast and it's all too easy to drift from one day to the next. Days turn to weeks turn to months and before you know it the year is over and those niggles, those itches, are no closer to being scratched.

The first step to being Youier then is setting clear and concrete goals based on those niggles because unless you really pay attention to those things that light you up, those things that get your heart racing, you're going to miss them.

Which leads us very neatly to your very first plaything, known as the "perfect ordinary day" exercise.

You're going to spend some time imagining what your "perfect ordinary day" would look like. It's "ordinary" because it's not your birthday. It's not a holiday. You're not on vacation. It's an "ordinary" work day where you're showing up, being you, Youier you.

Now there are a couple of ground rules. The first is that there are no limits on time and space. Consider that all of heaven is at your disposal so as you imagine your perfect ordinary day, do so from a place of everything working out how you want it to. You could wake up in South Wales, have dinner in New York and deliver a keynote address at dinner in Kenya, for example.

I can almost hear what you're thinking … "but who's going to pick the kids up from school?!?"

This is about having fun and unlocking possibility, allowing yourself to dig into those things that really light you up. If you start putting limitations on your imagination because of childcare issues, you're going to find it more difficult to tap into what's really important to you. In other words, the first rule is that there are no rules!

Having told you that there are no rules, the second rule is that you actually need to do it. Don't just do this exercise in your head. Make time in your calendar to sit down with pen and paper. By all means go for a walk and ponder on it a little bit, but then sit down and write it - and be specific!

Where will you wake up? Who will you wake up with? What will you do? What will you have for breakfast? And then what will you do? And then what will you do? And then what will you do? How will being and having and doing these things make you feel? Where's the joy in the day? What brings a lightness to your step and causes you to loose all sense of time?

By being specific, you're going to unlock things that you didn't realise were important to you.

Having crafted your Perfect Ordinary Day, the next step is to break that down into smaller pieces which, candidly, is outside the remit of this one short chapter. But never fear, if you enjoyed this exercise and want to take it deeper, I'd highly recommend Youier Goal-Setting, my short little Kindle book, available for free via Amazon: GetBook.at/youiergoalsetting

Youier Productivity

Having established those things that are important to you and crafted goals you actually want to get done, another piece of your life where you can practice being Youier is getting stuff done or "productivity".

Now this isn't about hacks or systems or adding more pressure to your already over-anxious mind. This is simply about you getting stuff done in a way that works for you, honouring who you are and how you like to show up in the world.

Let me give you a concrete example …

I'm the kind of person who, when faced with a list that's too long (or even worse, feels never-ending!) will shut down. I get so easily overwhelmed, it's like my brain rejects all options in a bid to protect me.

Writing this chapter is a case in point. I had a deadline. Feeling overwhelmed, I negotiated a new deadline, such that it became a little bit further out. And then I made a promise, a commitment, that I would get my chapter done by a specific date.

Now, me being me and knowing myself as I do, one of the things I know I will not do is break a commitment but when I made this commitment, I did so forgetting that it was a week when I already had a lot on my plate. Birthdays, podcast recordings; the week got fuller and fuller and I found myself with a choice: go back and negotiate the deadline (again!) or experiment with a new way of getting stuff done, a way that helped my brain feel less overwhelmed and more amenable to doing the work!

And so that's what I did. Specifically, I experimented with speaking the first draft of this chapter into my phone and using Otter.ai to transcribe the audio. Now what you might not know about me is that I'm a total showoff so walking and talking this chapter into existence totally played into me being the person God made me to be.

Instead of slogging away at my desk on my own for hours and hours, I walked around the house, headphones in, imagining I was delivering this chapter to you as a keynote address. With my basic outline in place I was away! (Even that basic outline is a superb example of how being Youier, knowing how best you like to work, makes things easier.) It was great fun!

And that's what I want for you ... the freedom to get stuff done in a way that energises you and lights you up. Start thinking about what it looks like for you to get stuff done in a way that honours who you are.

Are you somebody who wakes up in the morning full of energy, ready to "eat the frog" as per Brian Tracy's advice? (As your resident vegan, I should add that no frogs were harmed in the writing of this chapter!) Maybe you thrive on getting that "one big task" done first?

Or do you prefer to start gently, get some easy wins under your belt first before tackling that big, audacious goal a little later in the day, after your second coffee?

Remember, there are no right or wrong ways to play with this. It's about getting stuff done in a way that's right for you. Start paying attention to those times in the day when you feel most energised. Where are you? When is it? Have you just eaten? Have you just had a cup of coffee? Are you sitting or are you standing?

And, by contrast, also pay attention to those times and situations in the day when you don't find it easy to get things done, when you're not full of energy.

We're human beings, we're not machines. There will be times when your body says, "rest" and I want you to honour that. There will also be times when you're feeling that resistance and not wanting to because your brain is trying to keep you safe. Don't be scared of the process, just remember there's a balance between resting and finding another way.

Here's the key though: until you really know yourself, it can be difficult to recognise the difference between needing to rest because you're tired versus resistance to the new, possibly scary, thing.

Which leads me to your Youier Productivity plaything: Start tracking your energy levels. Pay attention to the things that energise you and the things that don't.

Youier Wellbeing

I used to describe this as "Youier Mental Health" but this is about more than your mental health. This is about looking after all of you; body, soul, mind and spirit. They're all connected. You can't have one without the other.

But yet again this isn't about "one size fits all" solutions. This is about genuine self-care based on what makes you feel brilliant, not what you've been told should make you feel brilliant.

My classic example of this is journaling.

I am a writer and as a writer I write, a lot. I process my thoughts by putting pen to paper, so much so that there are often times that I don't really know what I think until I've formulated my thoughts into coherent sentences on the page.

But I have a deep, dark secret ... I don't like journalling! (Gasp!) I know I'm not meant to admit that out loud. I've read and can appreciate all the studies into how good journaling is for you but that doesn't change the fact that it really doesn't serve me.

Partly because I see my words as my gift to the world. Anything that takes those words and threatens to hide them away feels like a waste but it's more than just that. The other reason why I shy away from journalling is because my personality is such that I will fall down the rabbit hole of introspection and possibly resurface only days later! It serves no-one, least of all me.

And that really is the crux of the Youier message: figuring out what serves you, the person God made you to be. I can (and have!) given you examples from my perspective but considering this from other people's perspectives will only take you so far.

There are simply so many different things you can do that make you feel whole and happy, content and thriving. Just because something works for one person doesn't mean it will work for you. And conversely if something doesn't work for your best friend, it doesn't mean that you shouldn't give it a try. So start paying attention to those things that light you up whilst also noticing the "shoulds" that leave you feeling flat.

With all that said, this wouldn't be much of a section on wellbeing if I didn't introduce you to at least one or two fun playthings that, if you choose to use them, have the ability to quickly and easily turn your day around.

Silver-lining spotting

First up, it's what I like to call my "three word hack" for spotting the silver-lining in almost any situation. Are you ready for this? *insert drumroll* The three words are ... "But At Least".

Here's how we play with this: The very next time something happens that's less than wonderful, maybe it's something that's actually really irritating or frustrating, state the thing out loud, followed by the phrase "but at least" and then pause and allow your brain to fill in the blanks.

Your brain loves to fill in the blanks, it's just the way that we're wired. We simply don't like things being left unfinished. Don't believe me? Try singing the chorus of "Jingle Bells" but stop just before the very last word and pay attention to what happens in your body. See? Told you!

So let's turn that love of completion to our advantage and the very next time something difficult happens, force your brain to fill in the blank with the phrase, "but at least".

Say to yourself, "oh, that thing really sucked, but at least ... " and see what your brain comes up with. It's not a magic wand for tragedy, those times require a different kind of compassion, but most of the time life isn't tragic. Instead, most of the time life is full of niggles and irritations and things that make the day feel a little less lovely. Start playing with "but at least" and, before you know it, you'll be an irrepressible silver-lining spotter too!

Reticular Activating System (RAS)

And now it's time to gently introduce you to the cluster of neurones at the back of your brain that make up your reticular activating system.The reticular activating system does all kinds of wonderful things like regulate your temperature but, for the purposes of your wellbeing, it acts as a filter, filtering in (and out!) information.

Let's start with an example …

Think about the last time you bought a new car. (Let's pretend it's yellow.) And suddenly you start seeing yellow cars everywhere. Weird eh?! Or another classic example is when you or someone you care about is expecting a baby. All of a sudden there seems to be pregnant ladies everywhere! What just happened? Did your town really get flooded with pregnant ladies driving yellow cars or is there something else going on?

The answer is the reticular activating system. Instead of consciously processing every single piece of information that comes into your mind throughout the day, your reticular activating system filters in the things that are important to you. You buy a yellow car and suddenly start seeing yellow cars around town because your brain deems "yellow car" as of interest to you.

The Facebook algorithm acts a bit like a technological RAS. If your Facebook news feed delivered every single post from every single person you're friends with, every post from every single page you follow and all posts from every group of which you're a member, it would be stupidly overwhelming! Instead, the Facebook algorithm filters what it delivers based on the things you interact with online. Every time you "like" your best friend's cat memes, Facebook notices. When you scroll right past Uncle Joey's photos, Facebook notices. When you comment on your cousin's video, Facebook marks that action with a double star.

Now here's where it gets really interesting ...

Just like how you can "hack" your Facebook news feed by spending some time being thoughtful about what posts you interact with, you can absolutely "hack" your reticular activating system by teaching it what is important to you. How? Exactly the same way as Facebook .. by spending some time being thoughtful about how you respond to the things in your day that make you smile.

Have you ever seen an orange slug? I have, multiple times in fact, because I happened to see one once, years ago, and it amused me, so I stopped and took a good look at it. (It was almost neon orange. Who wouldn't want to look at something like that?!?) But that time spent looking at the slug told my brain that orange slugs are interesting to me so now it filters them in without me having to even think about it.

But now it's your turn to have a play with this. Take a look around you right now and consider, what's lovely? Or go outside and take a walk around your neighbourhood. Open your eyes. Pay attention to what you see. If you see something you find particularly delightful, pause and really look at it. Doing so signals to your brain that that is important to you and, over time, it'll start to filter in more of the same.

And just like silver-lining spotting, the more you do it the easier it becomes because your brain will start to help you out by filtering in more and more examples. It's the reason why, if you spill your morning coffee and you think to yourself, "oh no! My day is ruined!" your brain will filter in examples to prove you right but if you instead think, "ah well, the day can only get better from here!" it generally will. That's how powerful your amazing God-given brain is.

And there we have it, two quick and easy little bits of brain science that'll help you smile, almost right away. The secret is, you need to give them a try.

Youier Faith

The final area where I'm here to encourage you to be Youier is in your faith. Personally, my faith is centred on God's love as expressed through Jesus but, for the purposes of Youier Faith, the specifics of your faith system are largely irrelevant. Instead, Youier Faith is about substituting the "shoulds" of religion for a loving relationship with God.

Let's take a classic "should" I heard a lot about as a teenager in the church … prayer. Now don't get me wrong, I think talking to God is great but do you know what's not great? Using prayer as a tool for making the people God's loves feel small or inadequate. I used to feel so guilty. I'd sit in church every Sunday and promise God faithfully that this would be the week I'd pray and read my bible lots. And then Monday would happen and all those promises went out the window, until the next Sunday when we'd do the whole promises dance all over again!

Sure, prayer and reading the bible can be great for your faith but doing either from a sense of duty or because you think you "should" is no way to live. It was never part of God's plan. There's got to be a better way! Ultimately, it's about you being you, the person God made you to be, in every area of life, including how you "do" your relationship with Him.

If, like me, you're easily distracted, sitting in a quiet room will either cause your head to spin with hundreds of thoughts all demanding attention or, if you're particularly sleep-deprived, you'll fall asleep! Instead, I like to talk to God while I'm out walking the dogs. Being outside in nature always makes me feel closer to God anyway but it also seems to somehow slow down (and sometimes even stop!) my wandering thoughts.

The wonderful thing is God made you. Before you were even a twinkle in your mother's eye, He knew you, whispered dreams of you, saw all that you would be and could be. And because He made you, he knows who you are, the way you're wired. He knows how you interact with the world. So if He made you to be you and if He knows what you're like, why would He need you to do faith in any way other than the way that honours the person He created you to be?

The greatest thing you can do to really embrace who you were made to be, to really be

Youier, is to wake up each morning and say to God, "Good morning God, thank you for this brand new day! What are we going to do today?" And then step into that brand new day with Him, whatever that looks like within the context of you being you.

Maybe you're out walking your dogs and as you walk down the street you can be talking to God about the people in the houses, praying for them, even if you've never met them. Or when you step into a situation in your place of work, ask God to guide you in the potentially tricky conversation. Or when you sit down at your desk, ask God to help you. I do this when I write the daily notes for the members of my community, the Itchy Soul Playground. God knows what they need and I ask Him to lead my writing.

The more that you can be in relationship with God, every single day, whatever that looks like within the context of you being you, the better. That's ultimately what Youier Faith is about. It's about saying to God, "okay you made me, you know me. Show me what it looks like for me to be me. Show me what it looks like for me to step into this brand new day, full to the top with your love, fully self expressed."

Which leads us rather neatly into the plaything for this final section. It's about "love notes" and it ties in with the RAS that I introduced you to previously so you get two opportunities to practice playing for the price of one. Bargain!

Here's what I want you to do ... Ask God to help you see the love notes from Him in your day. What does a love note from God look like? Good question! These are things in the day that make you smile. Things that give you reason to pause because they're just lovely.

Some examples might help: One of my favourites is "cloud porn." (And nope, that's not naked photos stored "in the cloud"!) "Cloud porn" is how I describe what happens to the clouds when the sun is setting and it turns the sky orange and pink. It's just beautiful!

Other people find themselves overwhelmed by God's love when they look up at the sky on a cloudless night and see the stars dancing. For others it might be flowers or the laughter of a child or bird song.

Whatever those things are that make you pause and think, "Yes God, thank you, I know you love me.", those are love notes and I want to encourage you to ask God to help you see them more. And because of RAS, the more that you start to look out for those love notes, the easier it will become to see them.

So every time you see that sunrise, remember that God loves you. Every time you hear that little whisper on the breeze, say "thank you God, I know that you are there." It's a relationship, a two-way thing. And just like there's no "one size fits all" for goal-setting, productivity or wellbeing, the only "right" way to "do faith" is to be true to the person God made you to be.

Which leads us right back to where we started and I leave you with a choice because, as we identified at the very beginning of our time together, happiness might not be the polar opposite of anxiety but by increasing your day to day happiness, it'll make it easier for you to apply any of the other strategies and advice given in this book.

And so the choice ...

You being Youier is a journey but it starts with that cliched first step. And yes, it's a cliche, but it's a cliche because it's true. You can choose right now today to be you.

And yes, there will be days when you hide your light, there will be days when you're not true to the person that God made you to be but that's okay because this isn't about striving for the perfect score. You don't have to beat yourself up for the times you don't get it right. Instead, simply choose something and play with it. And remember, God loves you. You're His masterpiece, His creation, His work of art, and He does not need a do-over!

About El Edwards

Founder of the Itchy Soul Playground & Youier Media, El Edwards is on a mission to inspire you to live a life slap bang in the centre of God's love, to ask those questions you almost dare not ask. To be everything God had in mind for you when He dreamed you into existence with His love.

El wants to live in a world where silver-lining spotting is taught to all ten-year-olds, growing up is outlawed and laughter is the magic pill that cures all. To find out more about El and the Itchy Soul Playground, go to Youier.com/join

Using Ayurveda To Heal Anxiety
by Zeeba Khan

Ever since happiness heard your name, it has been running through the streets trying to find you.
-- 14th century Persian Sufi poet Hafez

More than 5,000 years ago, Indian sages developed Ayurveda, which continues to be one of the world's most powerful mind-body health systems. Ayurveda is a science of life ("Ayur" meaning life and "Veda" meaning science). The two main guiding principles of Ayurveda are 1) the mind and the body are interconnected, and 2) the mind is the most powerful tool to transform the body. There is no separation of the consequences of each one on the other. Ayurveda is holistic healing.

This ancient Indian system of medicine is based on the idea of balance in bodily systems and uses herbal treatments, yoga therapy, exercise, meditation, breathing exercises (pranayama), diet, and nutritional supplements to help people stay vibrant and healthy while realizing their full human potential.

Ayurveda teaches us that health is not merely the absence of disease, but rather that our natural state is one of health, happiness, and an inner sense of well-being. This is achieved when our body is clear of toxins, our mind is at peace, our emotions are calm and happy, our wastes are efficiently eliminated, and our organs are functioning normally. Ayurvedic healing is about balance, and the more we are balanced, the more we will be healthy.

Ayurveda is a personalized approach to health, and knowing our mind-body disposition allows us to make optimal choices about diet, exercise, nutritional supplements and all other aspects of our lifestyle. It teaches the art of mindful and conscious eating and how to incorporate it into our life by showing us that food not only tastes good, but is good for us. What we put into our body dictates the quality of our life. If we use food as medicine, we will be delightfully surprised at how much better we feel and how much more clearly we think.

Some Ayurvedic suggestions include:
- Eat a colorful, delicious diet to balance our doshas
- Get plenty of sleep
- Follow the rhythm of nature
- Move our body
- Stoke our digestive fire
- Relax

Basic Principles of Ayurveda

The basic principles of Ayurveda are that there are five great elements (or panch mahabhuta), three mind-body-spirit constitutions (or doshas), and seven body tissues (or dhatu). The five great elements are comprised of earth (prithvi), water (jal), fire (agni), air (vayu), and space (akaash). These five elements create three doshas.

Prithvi + Jal = Kapha
Jal + Agni = Pitta
Vayu + Akaash = Vata

The *Vedic* scriptures say that there is an inextricable link between humans and the Universe: "Yat Pinde, tat Brahmande." As is the Universe (macrocosm), so is within the human body (microcosm). The entire cosmos or Universe is part of one singular absolute. Everything that exists in the vast external Universe (macrocosm) also appears in the internal cosmos of the human body (microcosm).

Tridosha Theory

Based on our dosha, we exhibit different kinds of emotions, reactions, and character traits. Whatever dosha we are born with never changes.

Characteristics of Vata Dosha

Vata is movement both inside and outside the body. Those with too much Vata experience heart palpitations, loose motion, are fidgety, have rapid eye movement, move very quickly and are mentally spacey. Their goals, emotions, and physical movements change quickly. Those with too little Vata experience laziness and are idle.

- Creative, quick to learn and grasp new knowledge
- Slender, tall, fast-walker
- Tendency toward cold hands and feet, discomfort in cold climates
- Excitable, lively, fun personality; changeable moods
- High energy in short bursts
- Tendency to tire easily and to overexert
- Full of joy and enthusiasm when in balance
- Responds to stress with fear, worry, and anxiety, especially when out of balance
- Tendency to act on impulse
- Often have racing, disjointed thoughts
- Generally have dry skin and dry hair and don't perspire much

Characteristics of Pitta Dosha

Pitta is transformation, conversion, fire, heat, and intelligence. Those with too much Pitta experience difficulty in interacting with non-Pittas (because they perceive them to be slow thinkers and dumb), get angry quickly, have bad tempers, become aggressive very fast. They don't instruct; they demand. They are problem-solvers and execute plans, Type A personalities: they generate work, love to lead, tend to be the boss, face consequences, are very stressed, and are addicted to work. They are prone to diabetes, arthritis, dementia, and have too much gastric acid which can lead to gastrointestinal problems. Those with too little Pitta experience food poisoning.

- Medium physique, strong, well-built
- Sharp mind, good concentration powers, orderly, focused
- Assertive, self-confident, and entrepreneurial at their best
- Aggressive, demanding, pushy when out of balance
- Competitive, enjoy challenges
- Passionate and romantic

- Strong digestion, strong appetite, get irritated if they have to miss or wait for a meal
- When under stress, Pittas become irritated and angry
- Uncomfortable in sun or hot weather, heat makes them very tired, perspire a lot
- Good public speakers, generally good management and leadership ability, but can become authoritarian
- Subject to temper tantrums, impatience, and anger
- Typical physical problems include rashes or inflammations of the skin, acne, boils, skin cancer, ulcers, heartburn, acid stomach, insomnia, dry or burning eyes

Characteristics of Kapha Dosha

Kapha is the end product. Those with too much Kapha experience laziness, sluggishness, are heavy, overweight/obese, get stuck in life easily, and have a sedentary life in all aspects -- job, diet, lifestyle. They are prone to eye problems. Those with too little Kapha experience diabetes and allergies.

- Easy-going, relaxed, slow-paced

- Affectionate and loving, forgiving, compassionate, non-judgmental nature, stable and reliable, faithful
- Physically strong and with a sturdy, heavier build
- Slow speech, reflecting a deliberate thought process
- Slower to learn, but outstanding long-term memory
- Soft hair and skin, tendency to have large eyes and a low, soft voice
- Tend toward being overweight, may also suffer from sluggish digestion, prone to depression
- Gentle and essentially undemanding approach to life, very calm, strive to maintain harmony and peace in their surroundings, not easily upset and can be a point of stability for others
- Tend to be possessive and hold on to things, don't like cold, damp weather
- Physical problems include colds and congestion, sinus headaches, respiratory

problems including asthma, allergies, and atherosclerosis (hardening of the arteries)

Qualities of the Three Doshas

Although we contain elements of all three doshas, we tend to have a primary, secondary, and tertiary dosha. Our three doshas combine to form our prakruti, or our nature.

There are seven possible prakruti:
- Vata-Pitta-Kapha
- Vata-Kapha-Pitta
- Pitta-Vata-Kapha
- Pitta-Kapha-Vata
- Kapha-Vata-Pitta
- Kapha-Pitta-Vata
- Samaprakruti (all three doshas are balanced)

To live with optimal health, we must achieve balance between the body's constitutions of Vata, Pitta, and Kapha.

Three external reasons that cause the doshas to become imbalanced are:
- Weather
- Sensory overload or inadequate stimulation

- Unbalanced lifestyle (speaking too much and not listening enough, over-exercising or inadequate exercise, etc.)

Anxiety

Stress is our body's response when we believe that we do not have the adequate resources to deal with an internal or external need or threat. Emotions, thoughts, and feelings trigger stress and create a physiological reaction. Our sympathetic nervous system is our "on" switch. It triggers our fight-flight-or-freeze response and is given to us by nature. Our parasympathetic nervous system is our "off" switch. It activates our rest-relax-digest-heal response.

Anxiety is due primarily to the aggravation of Vata dosha in the nervous system. So to heal anxiety, we have to balance the Vata dosha by calming the sympathetic nervous system and activating the parasympathetic nervous system.

Our awareness can be a powerful agent for healing. A truly healing approach to time must be active, not passive. We need conscious responses, not unconscious reactions. The negative experiences that happened yesterday or years ago linger as memory or trauma. These wounds are the main obstacle to making every moment matter. Whenever we relive the past or become anxious about a painful future, we are allowing old wounds to take on new life.

A healing approach to time begins by noticing our reaction in the moment. When we are in a stressful situation or are reminded of painful experiences from our past, we need to take a few deep breaths and be aware of how we feel. We need to notice our emotions and how our body feels. We need to be aware of any instinctive reactions to resist, retaliate, or run away. We must recognize that those responses are coming from our past hurt. But our inner awareness, which notices these reactions and feelings, is not hurt or limited in any way by our past. This Conscious Presence is our real Self and it is the place from which we are free to choose a new response different from our conditioned response. As we become more familiar with remaining connected to our Conscious Self in stressful situations, we become free from our conditioned reactions and are able to more easily release our fear and anxiety.

Uncertainty is a fact of life. And yet in those moments when it suddenly sweeps into us, we feel anxious, stressed, overwhelmed and lost. In those moments of uncertainty, we begin to feel anxious because we begin imagining what the future will hold. We paint a dark picture where we believe that the next moment will be worse than this one. That we will be forced to experience unpleasant feelings that we want to resist having to feel. We fantasize about all the things that could happen and yet the truth is that we don't know what will happen.

Using Ayurvedic techniques, we can transcend uncertainty through a few basic techniques that will allow clarity to unfold so we can make better decisions, breathe more easily, and move through the day with greater grace.

Diet
Tastes of Ayurveda

As creation developed, it formed three underlying principles that uphold all life: the laws of creation, maintenance, and dissolution. Everything in life is born or created, it lives, and then it dies. These principles are known as sattva, rajas, and tamas, respectively, and are called the three gunas or psychological qualities. All of life follows these laws.

Food can be classified according to the trigunas. Sattvic food nourishes the mind, promotes intelligence, and balance. Rajasic food nourishes the ego, creates energy and causes imbalance. Tamasic food creates dullness, substance, and inertia.

- Sattvic: eating peacefully— vegetables, fruits, legumes, milk, ghee, honey, nuts, whole grains, beans, rice, herbal tea
- Rajasic: eating too quickly— coffee, caffeinated teas, soda, energy drinks, chocolate, spicy foods, salty foods
- Tamasic: overeating— meat, onions, garlic, scallions, leeks, chives, mushrooms, alcohol, eggplants, leftovers, fried food, canned food, frozen food

Food Plan to Balance Vata Dosha
- Eat more pungent, sour, and salty tastes
- Eat breakfast
- Warm food, very little cold or raw
- Moderately heavy textures, added healthy fats/butter
- Warm milk, cream, butter, soups, stews, hot cereals, fresh bread, hot drinks, herbal teas
- No caffeine
- Eat salted nuts
- Eat honey
- Eat wet foods, stay away from dry foods
- Eat root vegetables

Physical Treatment
- Nasya (clearing of the nasal passages). Begin with 1 teaspoon of salt mixed into

warm water. Lean forward over a sink, turning the head to one side over the sink, keeping the forehead at the same height as the chin, and ear parallel to the ground. Insert the neti pot into the upper nostril so that the saline solution flows in through the upper nostril and out of the lower nostril. Breathe through the mouth. When the neti pot is empty, face the sink and exhale vigorously while shutting the ears. Repeat the process on the other side.
- Abhyanga, or self-massage, soothes the nerves. Massage warm sesame oil, slowly and gently, over the entire body including the soles of the feet.

Meditation

Meditation can be done anywhere, at any time, lying down, sitting, or walking. Mantras, thoughts, feelings, looking at nature, thinking about God, love, virtually anything that doesn't cause strain or worry are acceptable forms of meditation. Practice giving up worry, fear, negativity, anxiety, and lack of faith. Knowledge and devotion are the most important aspects to practice.

Case Study

When Charlotte came to see me, she was 5½ months pregnant with her fourth child. Her obstetrician/gynecologist had told her that due to her hyperthyroidism (Graves' disease), she had a very high chance of miscarrying the baby or that the baby would be born prematurely. She has also been experiencing tachycardia, heart palpitations, hand tremors, and weight loss.

For her hyperthyroidism, Charlotte was instructed to have weekly treatments consisting of thyroid strengthening and meditation.

Herbal supplements were prescribed to regulate her endocrine system, to stabilize her metabolism, to increase her ability to handle stress and to calm her nerves: meshashringi and brahmi.

Charlotte was advised to consume sattvic food. These foods increase life, vitality, purity, strength, balance, stamina, health, happiness, and cheerfulness.

Physical treatment of Charlotte's thyroid and the ensuing anxiety involved the use of an Ayurvedic tonic to reduce inflammation, rejuvenate the thyroid, and improve its quality. Hot/cold therapy and chanting were also included.

Mind Sound Resonance Technique

The Mind Sound Resonance Technique (MSRT) is a meditation that involves two kinds of chanting – ahata (aloud) and anahata (mental chanting, chanting silently to oneself).

MSRT begins with the Maha Mrityunjaya Mantra, also known as the Great Death-Conquering Mantra, recited in Sanskrit as the opening prayer.

Om Tryambakam yajaamahe
Sugandhim pushti vardhanam
Urvaarukamiva bandhanaan
Mrityor mukshiiya maa amraatat
Om, Shanti Shanti Shanti

This translates into:

We meditate on the three-eyed reality that is God,

Which permeates and nourishes all like a fragrance.

May we be liberated from death for the sake of union with God,

Just as the cucumber is severed from bondage to the creeper.

Om, Peace Peace Peace.

Following my instructions, Charlotte chanted "A," "U," "M," "AUM" sometimes alone and sometimes with me. We meditated on God. We fell into silence, and Charlotte concluded the practice by planting the seed of a positive resolve.

MSRT ends with a prayer, recited in Sanskrit, from the Upanishads.

Sarve bhavantu sukhinath
Sarve santu niramayah
Sarve bhadrani pashyantu
Ma kakshit dhukh bhagbhavet
Om, Shanti Shanti Shanti

This translates into:
May all be happy.
May all be free from illness.
May all see what is spiritually uplifting.
May no one suffer.
Om, Peace Peace Peace.

At the end of each of our sessions, Charlotte's heart rate had often fallen at least 10 beats per minute, from the high 80's to the mid- to low-70's. She felt calm and had no traces of anxiety.

Through her meditation practice, Charlotte learned to withdraw to her inner refuge of total bliss, peace, and rest. She began to feel more positive about life and gain more self-confidence as a result of her thyroid returning to normal functioning levels. She even reported an improvement in her relationship with her spouse as well as her children.

With regular practice, Charlotte was able to reverse her hyperthyroidism, be free from anxiety, and wean off her medication.

Mantra
Ram

Our third chakra, the solar plexus chakra, is at the center of our torso, the center of our body. In Sanskrit, the solar plexus is called the Manipura chakra. The Mahabhuta, the element, is fire. This is our transformation center, our intention, our desire, our manifestation center, your follow-through. The vibration for this chakra is "Ram" and the mantra is "I do."

Practice:

1. Sit with your back erect in a comfortable seated position.
2. Gently close your eyes.
3. Place your palms up on your knees.
4. Pay attention to your breath. Let your lungs breathe with no effort on your part.
5. Silently repeat "Ram."
6. Start with 5 minutes of silent chanting followed by 10 minutes of silent meditation.

So Hum

According to both Hindu and Buddhist traditions, the So Hum mantra is considered to be the vibration of the cosmic unheard AUM and produces a union between the individual and Universal Consciousness.

"So Hum" is translated as "I Am That." Hum means "I" or the individual ego. So means "the Divine." We inhale prana, or the life force energy, and we exhale our ego.

It is best practiced in the early morning or late at night on an empty stomach.

Practice:

1. Sit with your back erect in a comfortable seated position.

2. Gently close your eyes.

3. Place your palms up on your knees.

4. Pay attention to your breath. Let your lungs breathe with no effort on your part.

5. On the inhale, silently say "So."

6. On the exhale, silently say "Hum."

7. Start with 5 minutes of silent chanting followed by 10 minutes of silent meditation.

Herbs

- Asafoetida (Hing)
- Ashwagandha
- Brahmi
- Calamus

- Cardamom
- Chamomile
- Cinnamon
- Cloves (Laung)
- Coriander
- Cumin (Zeera)
- Fennel
- Fenugreek (Methi)
- Ginger
- Indian holy basil (Tulsi)
- Lily
- Nutmeg
- Rock salt
- Sandalwood (Chandan)
- Almond milk with pinches of ginger, nutmeg, and saffron
- Orange juice with a teaspoonful of honey and a pinch of nutmeg

Exercise

Vata-pacifying exercises include walking, tai chi, chi gong, swimming (be sure to avoid becoming chilled), gentle cycling, and Vata-pacifying yoga such as restorative yoga.

Yoga Asana
- Shavasana (corpse pose) is also useful when practiced between asanas, and after a stressful day.

- Sitting and prone positions are also beneficial. Shoulder stands and back bends are also helpful if there are no heart problems. Deep breathing promotes calming.
- Vipreet karani (Legs-Up-the-Wall Pose)

Practice:

1. Find a wall space that is clean and clear. Gather two blankets, a belt, and two eye pillows. If you have a bolster, bring that along.

2. Fold one blanket into a large square. Then fold that in thirds, creating a firm, supportive cushion. Place your blanket cushion about 12 inches away from the wall.

3. Fold the other blanket in half and place it three feet from the wall. You'll use this blanket to support your head and to fill in the space between your neck and the floor.

4. Sit sidesaddle on the cushion so that your right side is near the wall. Loop your yoga belt around the middle of your shins. Draw it snug but not tight.

5. Place your left elbow on the floor and swing your legs up the wall. The rest of your body will naturally go down so that you end up lying on the floor with your legs up the wall.

Aromatherapy

Diffuse essential oils of sandalwood, lotus, or sacred frankincense to calm the nerves.

Pressure Point

Make a fist with your left hand. Locate the point where the tip of the middle finger touches the palm. Take your right thumb and press firmly on this point on your left palm for about 1 minute. This will calm down the agitation of prana, which causes anxiety.

Pranayama

Bhramarí Kumbhaka (Humming Bee Breath)

Bhramri Pranayama is also known as Humming Bee Breathing.

The Bhramri pranayama breathing technique derives its name from the black Indian bee called Bhramari. Bhramri pranayama is effective in instantly calming down the mind. It is one of the best breathing exercises to free the mind of agitation, frustration or anxiety and get rid of anger to a great extent.

The exhalation in this pranayama resembles the typical humming sound of a bee, which explains why it is named so.

Bhramri has tremendous therapeutic potential. Like other pranayama, its power comes partly from its effects on the autonomic nervous system. Lengthening the exhalation relative to the inhalation activates the calming parasympathetic nervous system. For those who suffer from anxiety, the practice can begin to quiet the mind within a few breaths. The noise of Bhramari's incessant buzzing can drown out the endless mental tape loops that can fuel emotional suffering, at least for a few minutes, making it a useful starting point for those whose minds are too "busy" to meditate.

Bhramri pranayama works on calming the nerves and soothes them especially around the brain and forehead. The humming sound vibrations have a natural calming effect.

It is best practiced in the early morning or late at night on an empty stomach.

Practice:
1. Sit with your back erect in a comfortable seated position.
2. Gently close your eyes.
3. Keep your facial muscles loose, your lips lightly touching, and your jaw relaxed, with the upper and lower rows of teeth slightly separated.
4. Press the cartilage of both ears closed.
5. Keep the mouth closed throughout the practice.

6. Take a deep breath in. Observe the sensations in the body and the quietness within.

7. When you're ready, inhale and then, for the entire length of your exhalation, make a low- to medium-pitched humming sound in the throat. Notice how the sound waves gently vibrate your tongue, teeth, and sinuses. Imagine the sound is vibrating your entire brain (it really is).

8. Do this practice for six rounds of breath and then, keeping your eyes closed, lower your hands, and return to your normal breathing. Notice if anything has changed.

Alternative Practice (with Shanmukhi Mudra)

Press the cartilage of both ears closed. Close the eyes and lightly touch the inner corners of the eyes with the index fingers. Place the middle fingers on either side of the nose. The ring fingers are placed above the mouth, and the little fingers below the mouth.

Chandra Anulom Vilom

Nadi Shodhan Pranayama is also known as alternate nostril breathing. It is a practice used to purify the entire nervous system. It brings both the sympathetic nervous system and the parasympathetic nervous system into balance.

Chandra Anulom Vilom Pranayama, in particular, activates the parasympathetic nervous system and guides the body into a love state of being. It is very soothing, relaxing, and calming.

Practice:

1. Sit in any comfortable meditative posture that you can hold for a few minutes without any strain.

2. Keep your back erect.

3. Gently close your eyes.

4. Inhale deeply.

5. Exhale completely.

6. Close your right nostril with your right thumb.

7. Inhale deeply through the left nostril.

8. Exhale slowly and completely through the left nostril.

9. This is one round. Repeat for 9 rounds.

If you have practiced your Chandra Anulom Vilom correctly, you should feel fresh, energetic, relaxed, calm, and there should be a lightness to your body and mind.

Balance Leads to Happiness

People who are lonely, depressed, or isolated are 3 to 10 times more likely to fall sick and die prematurely from disease than people who are more connected to a community. Have people in your life who reflect your capacity to learn and change and grow in a positive way. Having positive relationships makes us feel empowered and accepted and also leads to fewer health issues.

Balance between the mind, body, and Consciousness leads to inner happiness. Happiness is not dependent on one single thing. Happiness is pure beauty, pure love. The mind is not merely a function of the brain; the body itself is a crystallization of mental patterns. Breakdowns in physical bodily functioning can lead to disturbances in the mind.

As the American philosopher Dr. Wayne Dyer said, "When you change the way you look at things, the things you look at change."

Try relabelling your way to grateful living. Practice seeing everything as a blessing and find a life lesson in it. Look at the next thing that you think you are going to receive as a blessing in disguise. It can really change our perspective, which in turn causes us to feel more optimistic about the future.

As we learn to balance the mind, the body will follow. When we are able to perpetuate physical changes, our mind sees its power and the process of self-realization begins. Ultimately, this is goal of good health.

What resonates with you? Choose something, one thing. Start slow and watch as your body-mind-spirit unfold into a blissful state of being.

Allow your *Best Version* to flow. Notice your Essence merging with the Divine.

Don't dwell on what can go wrong. Instead, focus on what to do next. Spend your energies on moving forward toward finding your next right action.

You are elastic and flexible in thought, heart and deed. You are able to change your opinion and step up to the world whenever you wish.

In any given moment, you have the ability to choose your thoughts. Choose the ones that make you feel good.

References:

Dimmitt, C. & van Buitenen, J. A. B. (Eds.). (1978). *Classical Hindu Mythology: A Reader in the Sanskrit Puranas. Philadelphia*, PA: Temple University Press.

Lad, V. (1998). *The Complete Book of Ayurvedic Home Remedies.* New York, NY: Harmony Books.

Tirtha, S. S. S. (1998). *The Ayurveda Encyclopedia: Natural Secrets to Healing, Prevention, and Longevity.* Bayville, NY: Ayurveda Holistic Center Press.

About Zeeba Khan

Zeeba is an internationally experienced Ayurvedic clinician, meditation teacher, energy healer and motivational speaker who uses holistic treatment to restore her patients' mental, physical, emotional, and spiritual health and to prevent disease and disorders.

She has presented month-long workshops to corporate clients, including some well-known global leaders. She has also led meditation and yoga workshops at schools internationally to incorporate wellness education into their curriculum. She has explored different types of non-religious and religion-based meditations and uses them as part of her treatments.

Zeeba was raised mainly in the United States but comes from a mixed heritage background. Her early career spanned modelling, acting, television, radio, and journalism before she entered academia and became a Professor in Communications to teach and research religious harmony across various interpersonal, organizational, and intercultural contexts.

She believes strongly that it is imperative to meditate, even in the good times, to build a silo of resilience so that when we are faced with challenges, we are not running on empty and are able to weather any storm.

Zeeba is trained and certified in the Ayurveda Sciences at Union Yoga Ayurveda, affiliated with Atreya Ayurvedic Medical College and the Indian Institute of Patanjali Yoga, associated with Swami Paramahansa Samsthana, and a registered member of the National Ayurvedic Medical Association, USA.

Learn more about Zeeba at www.zeebahealing.com and on Instagram @zeebahealing.

Now What?

Your journey with *Anxiety And Us* doesn't end here. Whilst we've introduced you to different modalities for dealing with anxiety, this isn't the end of the story. Come and join the private Facebook group where you can meet the authors, ask questions, download resources to accompany the book - and much, much more!

www.bit.ly/AndUsFacebookGroup

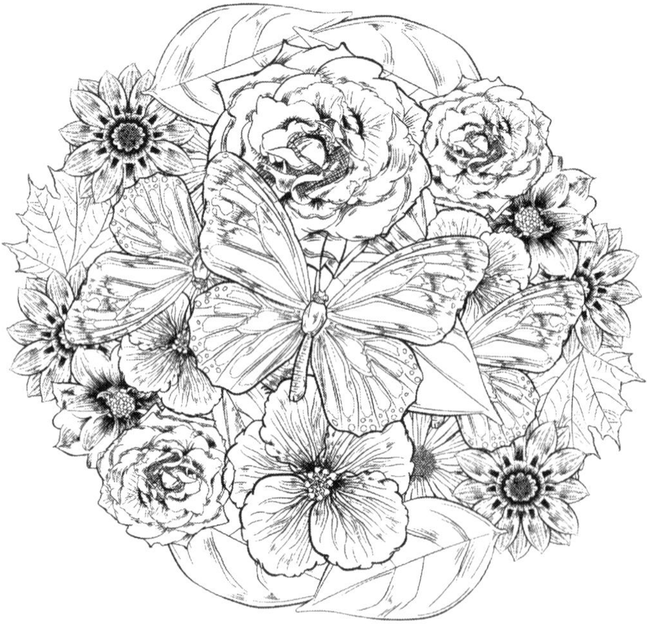

Sadness And Us

If you enjoyed Anxiety And Us, you'll be delighted to hear the next book in the "And Us" series, *Sadness And Us*, is due for publication December 2020, just in time for Christmas!

With stories of grief and loss, personal coping strategies for battling depression and bipolar disorder, and much more, *Sadness And Us* is here to help you appreciate the essential sweetness of life, move forward with confidence and function to the fullest with a constructive mental and emotional state.

To be one of the first to hear when Sadness And Us is ready for publication, follow Carolyn's Facebook business page, *Holistic Coach SG*

Acknowledgments

To all of us authors who overcame our own anxieties, personal battles and adversities including first-timer's and writer's anxiety to contribute generously from their hearts to this project for the highest good. We are from an amazingly diverse range of backgrounds and walks of life. Although most of us were strangers at the start, some still are, we marvel at the commonalities in our purposes and desire to make a difference. Feel free to find out more about us as a group or individuals by contacting us.

To the authors and supporters who went the extra mile to help put this together in various ways by sharing their amazing skills: special shoutout to El Edwards, Martin Seville, Didi Kan, Hayley Amanda Hammer, Kellie Ahl from the UK.

Zeeba Khan, Stephanie Fam, Sean JW, Mohd Hijazi, Maybelline Tan and Anne Phey with Fauziah Shah, Dewi Adrini, Wiwiek Najihah and Janet Chui from Singapore, Birdy Diamond and Donna Maukonen from the US Ruth Sullivan and Jenny Schmal from the 'Your Authority Book' and other groups.

To Carolyn, for casting the net out and collating and helping craft and edit the authors' marvellous contributions. For coordinating this project which has become the first of its kind in terms of the diversity of authors and its cross-continental features.

And foremostly to El and Youier Media for the brilliance, the guidance and the patience in making it a reality.

The book is here, for real and it was birthed in one of the most stressful times for the planet. Look out for upcoming volumes!

Youier Media

"What we want is not more little books about Christianity, but more little books by Christians on other subjects - with their Christianity latent."
- CS Lewis

Youier Media is the publishing arm of the Youier, aimed at helping authors write and publish books in a way that honours who God created them to be. In essence ... Youier!

Established in 2015 by Itchy Soul Playground founder El Edwards, the goal then was quite simply to "scratch an itch" and that's as true today as it was back then.

Those itches or niggles to write a book? What if they were God's way of trying to get your attention? (Spoiler alert: If something's important to you, it's important to Him!)

Whether you need 1 on 1 accountability to get your first draft done via El's Playground Plus Voxer coaching or you have your book "done" and you're ready to take the next step towards getting it published, Youier Media is here to help!

Copyright © 2020 by Carolyn Street

All rights reserved. This book or any portion thereof may not be reproduced or used in any manner whatsoever without the express written permission of the publisher except for the use of brief quotations in a book review or scholarly journal.

First Printing: 2020

ISBN 9781999710699

Youier Media
80 Queen Victoria Road
Llanelli, SA15 2TH
YouierMedia.com